THIS CHANGES EVERYTHING

Transforming Your Life From the Inside Out

Jaya Koilpillai Bohlmann

MA, APR, MSMOB

This Changes Everything: Transforming Your Life From the Inside Out

Copyright © 2017 Jaya Koilpillai Bohlmann

All rights reserved.

ISBN: 0692296921

ISBN 13: 9780692296929

Library of Congress Control Number: 2016907124

Jaya Bohlmann, Olney, Md.

**THERE IS NOTHING AS TIMELESS,
YET EVER-CHANGING, AS NATURE.**

Dedication	*viii*
Introduction	*ix*
Using This Book	*xi*
About the Designing Change Model	*xii*

1. UNDERSTANDING CHANGE 1
    - You as A System 3
    - Emotional Stages of Change 7
2. KNOWING YOURSELF 10
    - The Johari Window 12
    - Feedback 13
    - Values 15
    - Passion 18
3. KNOWING AND MANAGING OTHERS 20
    - Managing People 21
    - Listening 23
    - Keys to Active Listening 24
    - Relationships 27
4. BRIDGE TO THE FUTURE 30
    - Forgiveness 31
    - Gratitude 36
5. MOVING FORWARD 40
    - Value Proposition 41
    - Setting Goals 43
    - Time Management 45
6. BE YOUR OWN CHANGE 47
    - Ban the Shoulds 48
    - Reframing 50
    - The Physical Requirements of Change 54
7. UNDERSTANDING AND MANAGING THE STRESS OF CHANGE 57
    - Stress and your Body 60
    - Just Breathe 63
    - Just Move 64
        - Morning Exercises 67
    - Get Outside 71
    - Eating for Stress Management 75

Mind Over Matter	79
A Change Friendly Environment	84

8. INSPIRATION   94

References for Further Study   *97*
About the Author   *103*

JOURNEY HOME

The time that my journey takes is long and the way of it is long. I came out on the chariot of the first gleam of light, and pursued my voyage through the wildernesses of worlds, leaving my track on many a star and planet.

It is the most distant course that comes nearest to thyself, and that training is the most intricate which leads to the utter simplicity of a tune.

The traveler has to knock at every alien door to come to his own, and one has to wander through all the outer worlds to reach the innermost shrine at the end.

My eyes strayed far and wide before I shut them and said "Here art thou!" The question and the cry "Oh, where?" melt into tears of a thousand streams and deluge the world with the flood of the assurance "I am!"

—Rabindranath Tagore

DEDICATION

For my colleagues, who give of themselves as professionals on a personal level, making this world more aware, authentic, and credible.

For my friends, who constantly communicate their belief in my chosen path, reminding me from where I've come and the bright places I'm heading.

For my sisters, and for my extended family, who create their worlds with brilliance, courage, and perseverance. Your love has opened many doors for me.

For my parents, who left behind safety and familiarity for new shores and a life constantly expanding in a huge, generous embrace of the world. You show me that an adventurous life is the only one worth living, and that faith is the path as well as the destination.

For my gifted husband, who has courageously adopted a new career, owning his calling and passion for healing the world through science, nature, and the inherent wisdom of all humans. Your devotion and skill inspire me, and your love is the shining light of my future.

For my beautiful daughter, who believes in everything I do. You are the purest form of love there could ever be.

THIS CHANGES EVERYTHING IS FOR YOU.

INTRODUCTION

We don't change for the sake of change—we change for the sake of progress.

Although we strive for stability, predictability, and constancy, life is, by nature and design, one transition after another. Ocean tides ebb and flow; weather patterns fluctuate; and plants grow, wither, change, and die in the course of a few hours. Every second, trillions of cells in our own bodies are changing, dying, and being replaced in persistent patterns to adapt to stimulating conditions.

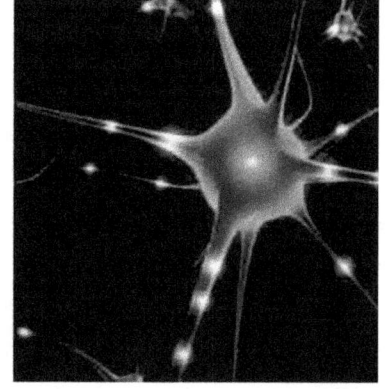

It's amazing to think about our bodies as change agents. The cells lining the stomach last only five days before being replaced. The epidermis—the surface layer of the skin—is recycled every two weeks or so. The entire human skeleton is thought to be replaced every ten years in adults, as bone-dissolving and bone-rebuilding cells combine to remodel it.

Change is literally in our DNA. We are made for change, yet many of us still actively resist it, clinging to the familiar even when it's not what we want. We resist change because we feel circumstances are out of our control, we don't understand it, or we just fear the unknown. Often, we don't feel capable of change, thinking its price outweighs any potential reward.

Since change is programmed in us and the world is constantly moving, it makes good sense that we learn how to keep up. Facing change doesn't have to be hopeless or overwhelming. You don't need all the answers, tremendous energy, will, or courage—not all at once anyway. You do need a prescribed path. You need a plan.

Whatever your relationship with change, this book will show you how to make your journey manageable, empowering, and focused on your goals. There is reward ahead.

USING THIS BOOK

One of the great discoveries a man makes, one of his great surprises, is to find he can do what he was afraid he couldn't do.
—Henry Ford

This book is designed to inspire and guide you through any personal changes you are facing. I recommend that you read the book in its entirety first, then reread the chapters most relevant to your current situation. Reflect on and complete the exercises; the worksheets at communication-leadership-change.com can help. I recommend repeating the exercises several times during your change process.

I also encourage you to record your change experience. This supports and enhances the change journey, whether through journal writing, audio or video recording, social media, or whether you choose visual or written methods.

This Changes Everything begins by describing the basics of some of the theories guiding the field of organization development (OD and behavior. Applying these to the phenomenon of personal change, I have created the Designing Change model, five stages of personal change that serve as the theoretical framework for this book. (Read more about the model in the next section.)

Next (chapters 2–4), you learn how to lay the groundwork for your personal change through an understanding of self and others (values, passions, feedback, listening, forgiveness, and gratitude). This awareness informs the creation of your change road map. You learn how to bring your change to life in chapters 5 and 6, as you create a value proposition, set goals, and organize your mind and resources. Taking care of your body, mind, and environment is the focus of chapters 7 and 8, along with inspirational quotes.

This last section contains basic information about mental and physical health provided by my contributor, Dr. John Bohlmann, based on his study of naturopathic medicine. We present some of the health topics we feel are most important to the change experience. The information is not intended as official medical advice. Please remember that anything you adopt as part of your health routine should be under the advice of your physician.

About the Designing Change Model

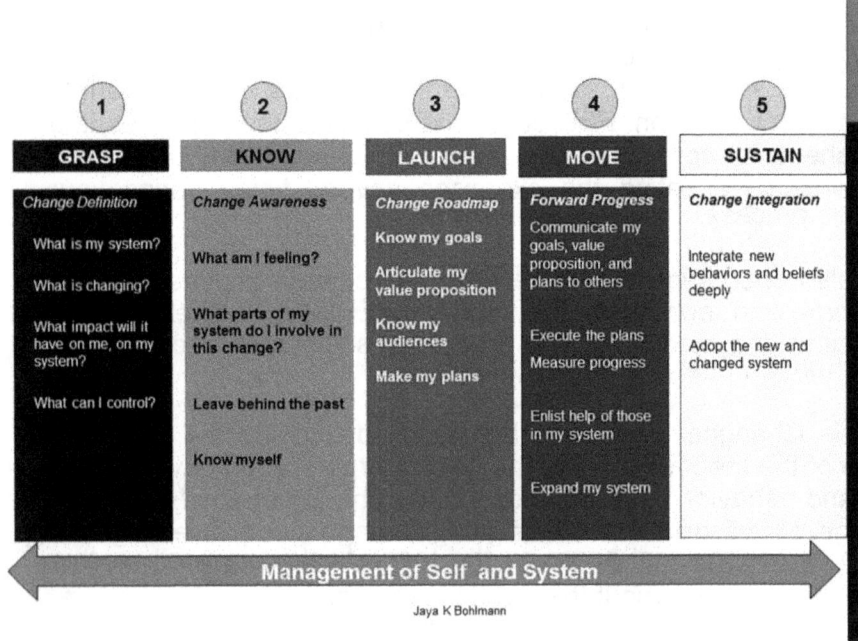

I created the Designing Change model to give my clients a road map for their change journeys so that they could chart their individual course for change and find a consistent cadence of progress toward their ultimate goals. In my experience, this kind of visual depiction can be a powerful ally to any major initiative, helping to provide the strategic plan that is essential to any type of success.

The model is the product of my desire to put change within both creative and scientific contexts. My intent is to describe the change process as a continuum of distinct, related, and interactive phases.

Broadly described, the Designing Change model takes the person undergoing change from realizing change is needed or happening, through processing and planning, and to the desired end state, or "new normal," via five distinct and related stages.

In addition to serving as a practical guide, the Designing Change model seeks to further an understanding of change theory—that is, the best ways to affect change within an organization, a person, or any human system.

I certainly stand on the shoulders of giants in creating the Designing Change model, as I've built it based on theories of pioneers and leaders in organization development (OD), behavior, change, psychology, communication, and other social sciences. These include Kurt Lewin and his three-stage "freezing" theory of change, John Kotter's eight-step change model, Warner Burke, Marvin Weisbord, Daniel Goleman, Therese Yaeger, Peter Sorensen,[1] and others with whom I studied during my graduate courses in organization development, communication, public relations, coaching, and leadership. I share this academic knowledge, enhanced with my real-life experience in leadership positions within companies and nonprofits, as a consultant and as an executive and personal coach.

I also share based on my own personal and professional experiences with change, which have run a full spectrum of cause and response—genetic and self-initiated, imposed by others, accepted with resignation, and embarked on with excitement. I am a second-generation Indian American. In a pioneer move, my parents left their native India and moved to the United States as young adults, raising my sisters and me in the suburbs of

Washington, DC, where I was born. They experienced many firsts during their four decades as US residents before moving back to south India twenty-five years ago to build and operate a nonprofit organization for abandoned children and provide health care for families—yet another landmark move. I grew up traveling across continents, especially the United States, marveling at beauty, history, family, genius, energy, and the spirit that drives people to sacrifice much to change the world, change themselves, and leave a legacy. I went to college in Canada and the United States, moved to Los Angeles after graduate school, and moved back to DC. After four years in Chicago, where my husband earned a doctorate degree in naturopathic medicine, we faced another big change as we moved to back to the Washington, DC area.

I know firsthand that the internal causes and effects of change are profound and that they must be the starting point. As a spouse and a mother, I have dealt with the emotions and pain of change and how it impacts those around you. I share this with you because we are all going through change, and although you can feel very alone, there are many traveling with you on the journey.

And change is certainly a journey. Lewin, a social psychology theorist and known as the father of OD[2] was one of the first to make the point that change is not an event but a process. He called that process a transition (the inner movement or journey we make in reaction to a change) and characterized it as unfreezing the existing state, moving toward the desired change, and then freezing the change at the new level.

Kotter[3], the renowned change scholar, agrees that change necessitates a series of phases that, in total, usually require a considerable amount of time.

The Designing Change model addresses change as the end result (the tangible difference in how we act and think today and how we want to act and think tomorrow) and transition as the process and art of getting there (shifting mind-set and managing our emotions so that we can safely and happily land in the new normal). I emphasize the emotional aspects of change because emotions are what fundamentally drive humans. I also discuss communication as the key to all successful change, whether personal or organizational.

1. UNDERSTANDING CHANGE

While change is the end state, transition is the act of changing—the process of getting there. One cannot happen without the other.

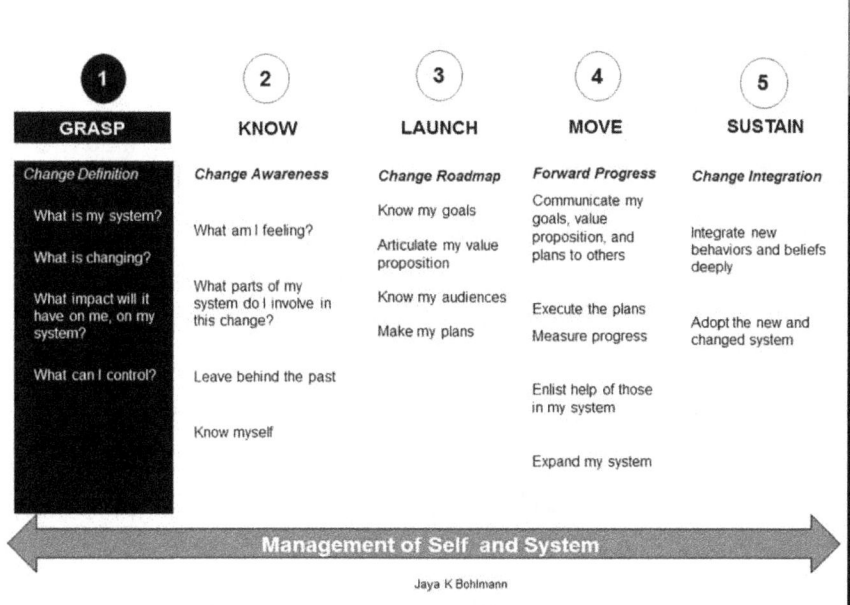

Changes can be internal (you initiate the change) or external (imposed on you by outside forces).

Internal: This includes a decision to lose weight, get a new job or a promotion, improve a relationship, be a more present parent, buy a house, start an exercise program, learn a new language, or take a trip—you get the idea. No one else is making you do it.

Although others might inspire or urge you, it's your decision to change. For example, your doctor asks you to lose weight or stop smoking, your new job requires you to learn a new language, or you take a trip at the request of family members.

External: This is change you don't initiate, is usually out of your control, and sometimes, is not what you want. This includes events like job loss, death of a loved one, or divorce.

Whether internally or externally initiated, change must be entered into as a deliberate process in order to be effective and successful. I have conceived the process of personal change to include five stages:

1. Grasp: We need to clearly understand the facts of the situation. Who is involved and impacted besides me? We focus on external facts.

2. Know: Beneath the facts, we deepen our self-understanding as it relates to the change situation. What led to the change? Did I cause the change or are others forcing it on me? How do I feel about this? How does this impact my values and goals?

3. Launch: With the foundation of understanding and knowledge, we create the structure of our change. Based on goals grounded in values and our deepest desires, we make our action plans.

4. Move: We move forward, executing the plans we've created.

5. Sustain: We take daily action so that the change becomes our new normal state.

This book presents guidance for your personal change journey according to these five stages. As you continue to read, remember that there is overlap in the stages, and they don't always proceed in a linear fashion. They should, however, progress all the way to stage five.

Hosur, Tamilnadu, India

You as a System

The myth of individualism ultimately is what drives us crazy. We need help. We need each other.

—Sukari Pinnock

A client came to me for coaching during an exciting and nerve-racking transition to a new job. This was a huge change for her since she had been happy with her previous employer for many years. In describing her transition to me, she talked a lot about the people in her life, and how they were impacted by her new job. For example, a relative had introduced her to her new boss, and others were glad to see her settled into a stable work structure. We set up a transition plan for her to navigate her new situation.

A few weeks into the new job, however, my client was in despair. She was finding most of the aspects of the new job intolerable, including her new boss. She realized that she had made a mistake, and my client wanted to correct it by leaving the job. But she was in agony about how to explain this situation to everyone without coming across like a failure or causing them to worry about her.

How would she handle their disappointment? What would they say? All of her focus was on them.

As we talked, my client came to realize that although she was right to be aware of the impact of her actions on the people connected to her—her system—she also needed to realize how her system impacted her. Were the people in her system encouraging her to make decisions that were authentic to her or were they concerned with their own feelings and goals? Were they trying to prevent her from changing in order to keep the system the same? My client came to realize that her first priority was to herself and that her system would indeed change, but not all of that change was within her control or her responsibility.

She made the decision to leave her new job and did so. Her system—the people around her—responded as she thought they would, and she was confidently ready to stand by her decision. Her system adjusted. Now she is happier than she's ever been, and her altered system is humming along again.

To understand personal change, it is helpful to use the lens of systems theory, which builds on the work of Austrian biologist Ludwig von Bertalanffy,[4] who studied the systemic interconnectedness of elements of nature in the 1950s. Social psychologists Daniel Katz and Robert L. Kahn[5] were among the first to adapt this perspective to organizational theory. "All social systems, including organizations, consist of the patterned activities of a number of individuals," they wrote in The Social Psychology of Organizations (1966, later revised).

This systems approach works well when thinking of people and change. We operate as individuals with interactions among other individuals, groups, and organizations as well as influences that have mutual impact and are in constant flux. In change, we have to consider our entire system. In my experience, frustrated or unsuccessful attempts to change are often when our systems are either inadequately included or unrealistically addressed.

Literature on biological and environmental systems says that the following key elements must be present and shared by all entities in order to be classified as a system:

- Shared Goal and Defined Objective: Every system has a predefined goal toward which it works. Businesses exist to sell products and services. Hospitals exist to provide medical care. A family exists to raise children. As an individual, what is the objective for a certain change? At the beginning stages, your objective might be to simply survive or stay above overwhelming emotions. As your change journey progresses, you will define a more meaningful, true change goal that has to do with what you want to become or accomplish.

- Standard of Performance: All the elements of a system share an acceptable level of performance.

- Environment: Every system, whether natural or man-made, coexists with an environment. It is very important for a system to adapt itself to its environment. You adapt to aspects of your environment every day—you alter your route to avoid traffic, you present your ideas to your boss to suit his or her style and expectations, and you wait to buy a house until interest rates improve.

- Feedback: Pay attention to friends, family, your community, and groups—how do they react to you? What are they telling you about yourself and themselves? This feedback helps your system meet standards and improve.

- Boundaries and Interfaces: Every system has defined boundaries within which it operates. Beyond these limits, the system has to interact with the other systems through interfaces. System users also interact with each other through interfaces. These connection points are important parts of systems; you need to know where you leave off and another element of your system begins. You need to know how they impact you and vice versa in order to manage the appropriate boundaries for each.

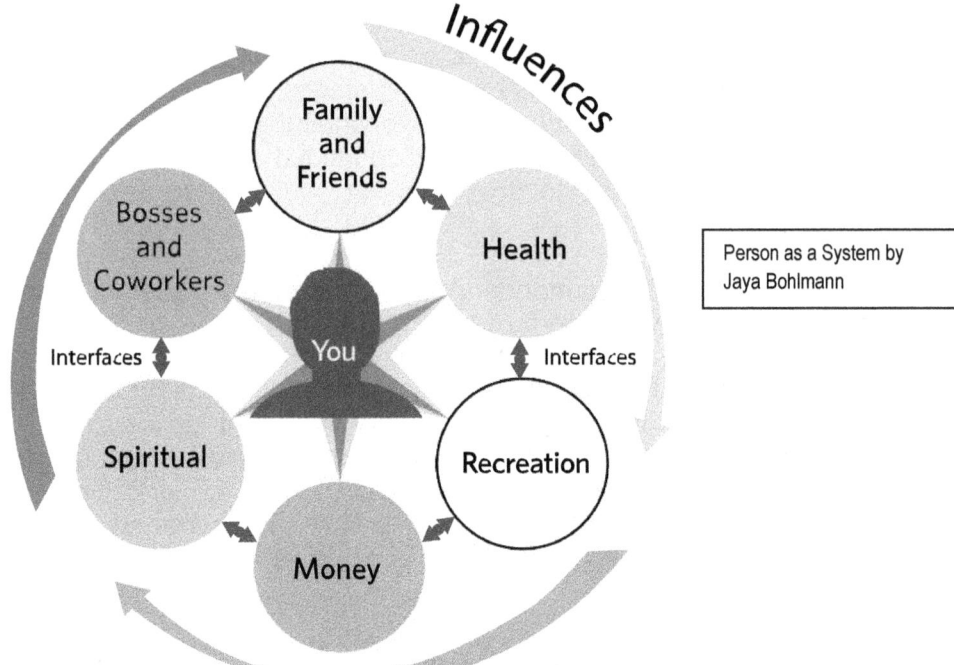

Get to know your system. Using the worksheet found at communication-leadership-change.com, describe and define your own system that is related to a change you are currently seeking. Keep in mind that while some elements of your personal system remain the same in all situations, others are situation specific. For example, your bank loan officer is part of your system in buying a new car but not necessarily part of your decision to get a new job. However, your spouse is probably part of your system for both types of situations.

Emotional Stages of Change

Events are always in flux. One day people love you; the next day you're their target. One day a situation is running smoothly; the next day chaos reigns. One day you feel like you're an okay person; the next day you feel like you're an utter failure. These changes in life are always going to happen; they're part of the human experience. What we can change, however is how we perceive them. And that shift in our perception is a miracle.

—Marianne Williamson

After a two-year search for a high-level corporate position, my client landed her ideal job. She was elated, relieved, and eager to begin and show the world her unique skills. She was also eager for the regular income and the chance to work with smart people and work toward a shared vision. After a month on the job, she called me to say something was "off." She didn't feel as happy as she thought she would. The sense of elation at landing the job was turning into something that felt like fear and doubt, even depression and sadness. What was happening?

Our emotions follow certain stages of change too, and these don't progress in a neat timeline to match the steps in a job search or any other transition. My client was still feeling some emotions related to the uncertainty, rejection, and loneliness of her job search. Once she understood that, she was able to be patient with herself and allow all her feelings to be expressed. In time, she felt much better and was fully able to embrace the great feelings that came along with realizing her dream.

While successfully transitioning to a new state of being requires taking certain actions, managing the transition also requires understanding your emotional responses. There is a progression of emotions commonly experienced during transition, which are related to my five stages of change.

In stage 1, when you're first faced with change and you're struggling to grasp what's happening and what it means, you might feel disoriented, confused, or in shock. You might be resistant. Your system has been hit, and all parts and connection points are shaken. Even if the change is for something good (you won the lottery, you lost twenty-five pounds, or you bought a new car), you experience the disorientation and disbelief that goes along with a body and mind that really want to keep things the ways they've always been. In change, we have to let go of things in order to make room for the new. That's a challenge when the old things were familiar, offering rewards that have been important to us.

At this stage, allow yourself time to understand and accept the change. Talk to trusted advisors, coaches, family members, friends, and coworkers—those who will listen to you with empathy and let you be open about your feelings without judgment. If you truly don't understand the change or why it's happening, talk to those who can answer your questions. Making logical sense of it all is the goal of this stage.

As you move to stage 2 and become more aware of your change situation, you are likely to protest, feel angry, or experience sadness. As time goes by and the change and its meaning sink in, you might start to experience feelings like resentment, anxiety, skepticism, or loss of a sense of status or identity. You might become depressed and listless—unable to process what's happening. Your morale might plummet. You might avoid people or become so negative that people don't want to be around you. It's all normal, and it's important to not get stuck here.

This stage can also be one of great creativity, innovation, and renewal. This is a great time to try new ways of thinking or working.

Moving to stage 3, you begin to prepare your structure and strategy for change. You might still feel overwhelmed, uncertain, or even anxious. It's understandable that by this time, you would feel tired. It's all normal. Also in this stage, you are called upon to act and move forward, even if you don't yet feel great. In fact, taking a few forward steps can help to stabilize your emotions. You've heard of "fake it till you make it" and "mind over matter." That's what we're talking about here.

This is the time to give yourself a strong sense of direction. Continue to talk with trusted advisors, especially those who can help you turn your goals into action plans while helping you deal with the emotions that naturally occur. Remember to be patient, as this stage can feel unproductive—you are planning and should not yet expect results.

The good news is that by stage 4, when you are taking specific change actions, you will start to feel acceptance, new energy, and excitement.

Moving to stage 5, where you're sustaining your change and creating your new normal, you will feel the satisfaction of seeing results, pride, and fulfillment in what you're accomplishing as well as enjoying the rewards of your efforts.

But we're trying to focus on taking action, moving forward, adapting our systems, right? Why get bogged down in the messiness of emotions? Because if we don't, they will bog us down. We are human systems, after all, not mechanical ones. We don't have operating systems; we have hearts, minds, and souls. Be aware of all your emotions during all five stages of your change.

I'm adapting concepts of organizational change to address personal change—some might say I'm taking liberties to do so. I believe both types of change are related. Personal change is the heart of organizational change. Organizations don't just change because of new systems, processes, or structures. They change because the people within the organization adapt and change. Only when the people within it have made their own personal transitions can an organization truly reap the benefits of change.

2. KNOWING YOURSELF

First, analyze yourself. Know yourself and your purposes. Know what you believe, physically mentally, spiritually. Know the sources of your beliefs. For in such an analysis you may find your true self.

—*Edgar Cayce*

A client of mine had made a dramatic career change—from artist to real-estate broker. She was excited about the shift, envisioning a career of matching people with their best new environments and making significant sums of money. Three years into it, neither of those goals were in sight. She'd been working hard and had taken the steps required in the real-estate profession—she just hadn't

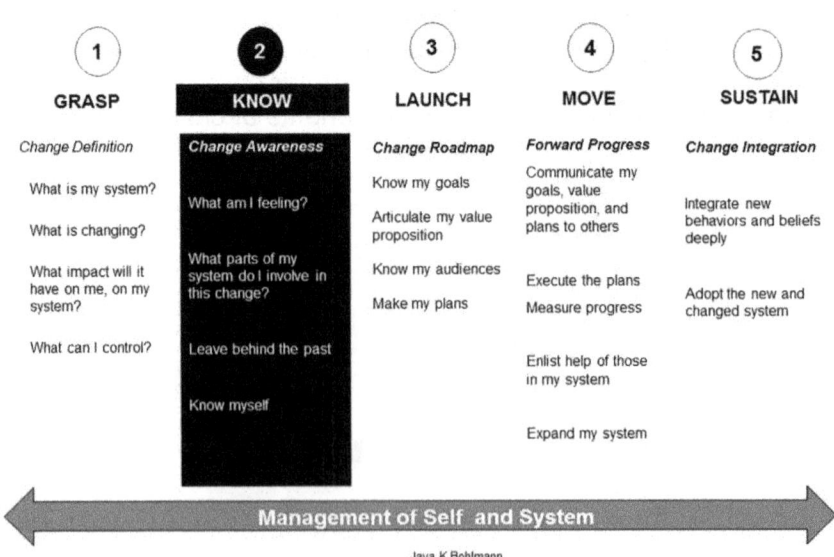

made any sales. She knew she "should" take certain additional actions to show her commitment to real estate, but she just couldn't seem to find the time and energy. We discussed possible reasons.

I often complete an exercise with my clients in which they go through a series of steps to compare the values they hold intellectually (the values they think they have) with their behaviors, which demonstrate our true values. Going through this values exercise with me, she realized that values one might typically associate with real estate (sales, competition, money, and buildings) were nowhere to be found on her list! With that realization, she was able to let herself off the hook. She didn't need to continue to pursue a career she didn't really feel aligned with. She could find ways to make money doing things closer to her true values.

While phase 1 of change asks us to understand the externals of our change, as we enter the second phase, we seek to deepen our understanding of our transition by going within ourselves in a reflective way with the goal of self-awareness.

I believe our true goal in life is to contribute what is unique and special about us and to offer the gifts only we can share. If each individual on this planet is unique, each of us can find the essence of that uniqueness as well as ways to give those things to the world. If we are born with a talent, a contagious passion, a special way of relating to people, a unique perspective, stellar leadership ability, or the ability to teach, it is our responsibility to share it. If we have any gift that helps, heals, honors, supports, or offers care for others, it is our mission to extend it. I believe we wouldn't be here at this time in history if not to use our gifts and talents.

With that in mind, we must first know makes us special! It's not always easy to discover this, and it's clear that we cannot do it alone. There is no such thing as perfect objectivity when it comes to self-evaluation. Mostly, we rely on feedback from others to know ourselves. This is a natural occurrence and how we gained basic knowledge and instinct from childhood. When we were children, how did we know that what we did or said was funny, helpful, or horrible? Because people around us laughed, applauded, or scolded.

The Johari Window

As we get older, people are less likely to give us such overt and proactive feedback about our behaviors. We have to find other tools to become self-aware. One such tool is the Johari Window model developed by American psychologists Joseph Luft and Harry Ingham in the 1950s.[6] It represents information—feelings, experience, views, attitudes, skills, intentions, and motivations—within or about a person. It looks at the information from four perspectives: open, hidden, blind, and unknown. The degree to which we share ourselves with others (disclosure) is the degree to which we can be known.

	Known to Self	⟷	Unknown to Self
Known to Others	Open	Ask questions	Blind
Unknown to Others	Hidden	Get feedback	Unknown

The Johari Window, Joseph Luft and Harry Ingham (1955)

• In the open area, people recognize us for the things we consciously know about ourselves. We move within this area with freedom and ease, comfortable that our actions and words are in alignment with what people expect from us.

• The hidden area contains those things we usually don't share. When we do, it is a deliberate choice we make only occasionally or with a select few people.

• When we operate in the blind area, we imagine things are true of ourselves, but these are not seen by others at all. If someone brings these qualities up to us, we might dismiss them outright. (However, if we are open to growth, we would solicit and accept feedback.)

- The unknown area contains those rich and complex elements that make us mysterious and interesting human beings. Neither we nor others are aware of these on a conscious level most of the time. Sometimes something from this unconscious area is revealed—often through deep self-study. This is the area in which we all need to constantly work.

A popular movie in my family is The Blind Side (Warner Bros, 2009), based on the true story of NFL offensive lineman Michael Oher and his amazing rise to football stardom. Oher is supported by a determined and strong adoptive mother, Leigh Anne Tuohy, (played by the award-winning actress Sandra Bullock). In one memorable scene, Tuohy motivates Oher to play more assertively by appealing to his protective nature, reminding him that his job is to protect his football teammates from opponents attacking their vulnerable blind sides. Seeing what his teammates cannot, he defends them for the good of the whole team, including himself. Oher applies the lesson to football and to his family, becoming a star and a role model.

Why is it important to limit what is unknown to us? Without the protection of awareness, we're walking around vulnerable, acting in ways that might not serve our goals or best interests. We cannot move with confidence, and we're forced to react rather than make the positive plays we really want. We might even get hurt. Your family and friends can fill in your blind spot through feedback.

Feedback

To know yourself and minimize your blind spot, solicit feedback regularly from people you trust to be honest with you. Whether in your personal or professional life, here are some techniques for doing this.

How to Solicit Feedback

1. Ask often. You can arrange for structured feedback sessions at regular intervals. More informally, ask for feedback about specific situations. At work, you could include feedback as part of regular meetings with your boss and subordinates. In your personal life, it's often easier to make this practice more situational, as in "How do you feel about the restaurant I chose?" "What about

the party did you like best?" or "How would you recommend I handle that differently next time?"

2.   Ask for comments on your behavior. "What can I do more of?" and "What can I do less of?" Ask these simple questions of your peers, bosses, and team members.

3.   Ask a varied audience. If you only ask one person for feedback, it might be worth hearing, but wait until you have more opinions before dramatically changing anything. Ask your fans and your enemies as well as your superiors and your direct reports. Listen for repeated themes. That's where your growth opportunities will be.

4. Be specific. The more you direct the feedback, the richer it will be. Maybe you have a goal in mind. You might say, "What do you think I need to do to be ready for a promotion in six months?" or "I'm concerned that no one is eating the kale-quinoa biscuits I made—can you help me understand this better?" Ask for the feedback that will help you understand or take action.

5.   Ask questions. If you're not sure how to direct the feedback, the following can be used as a script to gather broad, developmental feedback:

• I'm trying to be more effective in my role. What do you think I should start doing that I'm not doing now?

• What do you think I should stop doing that I am doing?

• What should I be sure to continue doing that you think is going well?

6.   Respond with "Thank you" or "Help me understand that." These responses will keep feedback channels open. It's not a two-way discussion at this point. If you start defending yourself against the feedback, stop. This practice is just about taking it all in.

Values

Values form the foundation of your life. They reflect the essence of who you are. Your values affect the way you think, the partner you choose, and, ultimately, the results you get in life. Knowing and understanding your core values allow you to use them as a reliable navigation system for your life—moving closer to the values that are most authentic to you.

What does it mean to live according to your values? It means feeling alive and energized. To start, it is important to understand what values are:

- Values are not morals. There is no sense of right and wrong in them.

- Values are not principles. They are not inherently virtuous nor are they standards of behavior.

- Values are the qualities of a life lived fully from the inside out.

- When we honor our values and the choices we make in our lives, we feel an internal rightness.

- Honoring our values is inherently fulfilling, even when it is hard. When we must suffer discomfort in order to live according to our values, the discomfort passes, and a sense of integrity and congruency with our values remains. When the values are not honored, we feel internal tension or dissonance.

- Values are intangible—they are not something we do or have. Money, for example, is not a value. However, being wealthy could be a value or using money as a means to fulfill other values (such as helping those in need) could mean that money has value for you but is not in itself a value.

- Although values are intangible, they are not invisible. People know your values by how you behave and the words you choose, if you're punctual or habitually late, what you find humorous and serious, and how you spend your money and time.

- Values are passionate.

- Values are not complex; they can be stated concisely.

Do you know your values? If it's been a while since you've thought about that, I've provided an exercise that can start you in the right direction.

From the following list, circle all the words and phrases that describe your values. Then do the exercise again, choosing only ten. It is this golden list of ten that you will focus on to create your change-related goals. (This exercise can also be found at communication-leadership-change.com.)

VALUES LIST

Honesty	Thoughtfulness	Diversity
Genuineness	Practicality	Travel
Authenticity	Nurture	Change
Accountability	Love	Movement
Directness	Beauty	New challenges
Sincerity	Romance	Opportunity
Strength	Freedom	Enthusiasm
Character	Exploration	Starting things
Stability	Creativity	Entrepreneurship
Sacrifice	Fun	Motivation
Legacy	Artistic	Progress
Family	Spontaneity	Inspiration
Marriage	Flexibility	Passion
Duty	Knowledge	Healing
Honor	Identity	Relationship
Heritage	The search	Team
Responsibility	Meaning	Community
Harmony	Influence	Belonging
Security	Truth	Pace

Passion

A life defined by dreams versus regrets generates an energy that is ageless. Dreams propel us forward with a childlike enthusiasm, transforming our perspective and framing a view of hope and optimism. We work to achieve our goals, but we chase after our dreams. Dreams often tap into our core beliefs, those things we would fight for and die for. History has proven that man will work for a dollar, but die for what he believes in.

—*Gary Friedman, Restoration Hardware*

As we gain clarity about our values, let's also be aware of those things that make us feel alive and energetic—those things for which we would sacrifice. These are our passions. While most of us are clear about what our obligations, needs, and duties are, we get less clear, especially over time, about our passions. Maybe we didn't think that we could make any money doing what we love, we thought that work and having fun are separate experiences, we were convinced we had to put our responsibilities ahead of our desires, or we were convinced that fulfilling our passions is a luxury, not within our reach, or even wrong. Times of change are excellent opportunities to tap back into what we love and to reconnect with what our hearts yearn for. Ask yourself the following questions and see if you can reconnect with your passionate self. (You can also complete the exercise at communication-leadership-change.com).

Passion Element 1: Energy

1. What three things can you not wait to get at each day? What three things do you dread and constantly want to avoid?

2. What things in life do you have a lot of energy for? Why? And where does the energy for them come from?

3. When have you had the most or least energy in your life? What were you doing in those times that energized or de-energized you?

4. What do you see around you that you want to fight for or against? What are you willing to pay a price for?

Passion Element 2: Fulfillment

5. What's been the most satisfying thing you've done? What made it so?

6. What gives you lasting satisfaction?

7. What have you done that you are most proud of?

8. What accomplishment or legacy would have ultimate significance for you?

9. What have you done in life that you'd love to do more of?

10. What makes you feel fully alive when you are doing it? What gives you the feeling of being right in the sweet spot of life?

Passion Element 3: Vision

11. If you could invest the rest of your life doing one thing, what would it be?

12. Imagine yourself at the end of your life and looking back. Is there a dream in you that would cause you regret if you didn't fulfill it?

13. In what ways would you change yourself, your family, your community, your health, and your business life if you could?

Remember, passion is about your emotions, not your thoughts. There are no right or wrong answers. Please ignore the "shoulds" in your head—rather, think about your energy, fulfillment, and vision as they truly occur in your life. Suspend judgment of your responses. Just answer.

3. KNOWING AND MANAGING OTHERS

The best time to plant a tree was twenty years ago. The second best time is now.

—*Chinese Proverb*

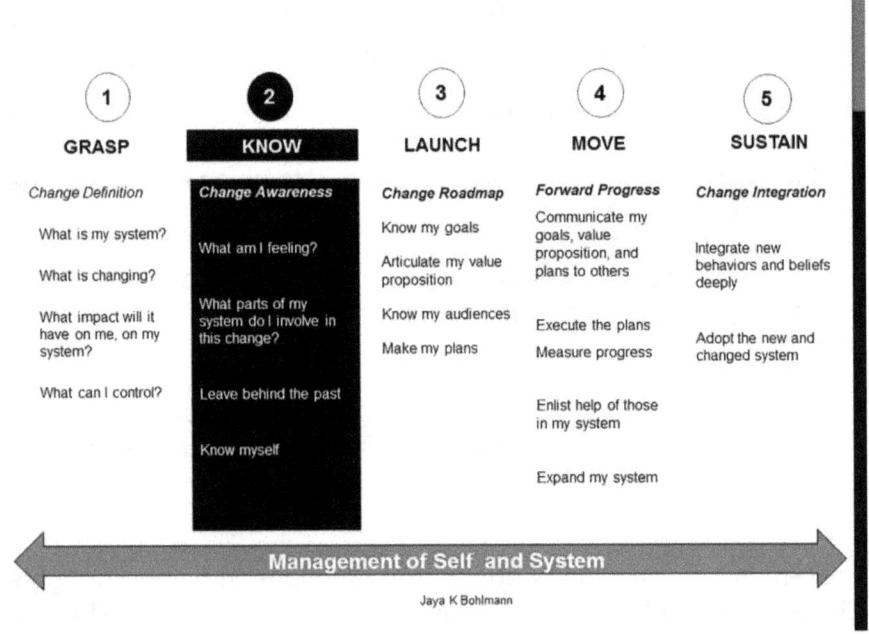

We are still in phase 2 of our change journey as we seek to understand others. This is important because although change is created from within, it's important to pay attention to other people as part of our systems. They impact us and our changes.

Managing People

For all the complexity of dealing with human beings, we share basic needs that can be handled with simple actions of grace and kindness. From Dale Carnegie's 1940s advice on how to win and influence people to Robert Fulghum's 1988 lessons learned in kindergarten,[7] the following advice for getting along with others is actually pretty easy:

• Smile.

• Remember people's names and use them.

• Become genuinely interested in other people and talk about their interests.

• Be a good listener. Encourage others to talk about themselves.

• Make the other person feel important, and do so sincerely. Give honest and sincere appreciation—not flattery. Genuinely find something about them to admire and express it enthusiastically.

• Don't criticize, condemn, or complain. Instead, find ways to build others up. If you must give negative feedback, do so privately and speak gently. Use encouragement. Make the fault seem easy to correct.

• Find out what the other person wants and align that with what you want.

• Don't argue. In arguments, someone must win and someone must lose. The losers lose face, self-esteem, and prestige—they won't do what you want in that state. Instead, find ways for both of you to win. Do this by understanding your opponents' opinions and find a middle ground, keep your temper, and, above all, listen.

• Show respect for others' opinions. If you differ, be kind and respectful in discussing the differences.

- Let the other person do a great deal of the talking.

- Let the other person feel the ideas are theirs.

- Try honestly to see things from the other person's point of view.

- Be sympathetic with the other person's ideas and desires.

- Make the person happy to do what you want. Show them how it benefits you. Be specific in your request. Be sincere and empathetic. Appeal to the nobler reasons people will help you.

The smartest person in the room isn't the most popular. The best-liked person is. While experience, education, and IQ can be the same among various individuals, charm, grace, and personality can make you stand out and get you more of what you want.

Hosur, Tamilnadu, India

Listening

Courage is what it takes to stand up and speak; courage is also what it takes to sit down and listen.

—*Winston Churchill*

A friend has repeatedly run into difficulty dealing with a series of bosses over the past six years. She feels she is doing her job at even higher standards than expected and is puzzled and pained when they or her team members find fault with her work product, her management style, or her communication approach. To try to correct this, she works herself harder and harder to get more and more done, thinking excellent work products will win back favor within the company. They don't, and she finds more responsibilities taken away from her, her salary cut, and her emotional and professional life suffering ever more.

What is happening? To figure it out, she parses and analyzes the words of her bosses and employees, trying to understand their instructions. She replays whole conversations in her mind and rereads e-mails to see where she might be going wrong in her interpretation of their expectations. She does this analysis after the fact—after the conversations in question have occurred.

Working together, we discovered one explanation for her confusion. In the moment of the interpersonal interaction, she is not listening well enough to the people around her. After going through some of the active-listening exercises I proposed, she is now better able to comprehend and retain what she is hearing from others. She is putting these new practices into play in a new professional role and feels happier with her business relationships.

Listening involves much more than hearing the words articulated. That is passive. Effective listening is active. It involves comprehending, retaining, and responding to the speaker.[8] Active listening is the practice of indicating that you both hear and understand what someone is saying, both intellectually and emotionally. For example, you might say, "If I'm understanding correctly, you're feeling frustrated that the board has put a tight deadline on the audit completion. Am I right?"

To become an excellent communicator, become an active listener.

Keys to Active Listening

Comprehend

Step 1: Face the speaker and maintain eye contact. In most Western cultures, eye contact is considered a basic ingredient of effective communication. When you talk, turn to face your conversational partners. Put aside papers, books, the phone, and other distractions. Look at them even if they don't look at you. Shyness, uncertainty, shame, guilt, or other emotions, along with cultural taboos, can inhibit eye contact for some people under certain circumstances. You can remember this about others, but stay focused on your own listening behaviors.

Step 2: Be attentive but relaxed. You don't have to stare fixedly at the other person. You can look away now and then. The important thing is to be attentive. Mentally screen out distractions, such as background activity and noise. In addition, try not to focus on the speaker's accent or speech mannerisms to the point where they become distractions. Finally, don't be distracted by your own thoughts, feelings, or biases.

Step 3: Pay attention to what isn't said—nonverbal cues. If you exclude e-mail, the majority of direct communication is probably nonverbal. We glean a great deal of information about each other without saying a word. Even over the telephone, you can learn almost as much about a person from the tone and cadence of his or her voice than from anything he or she says. When I talk to my best friend, it doesn't matter what we chat about—if I hear a lilt and laughter in her voice, I feel reassured that she's doing well.

Retain

Step 4: Keep an open mind. Listen without judging the other person or mentally criticizing the things he or she tells you. If what he or she says alarms you, go ahead and feel alarmed, but don't say to yourself, "Well, that was a stupid move." As soon as you indulge in judgmental thoughts, you've compromised your effectiveness as a listener. Listen without jumping to conclusions. Remember that the speaker is using language to represent the thoughts and feelings inside his or her brain. You don't know what those thoughts and feelings are, and the only way you'll find out is by listening.

Step 5: Create a picture of what the speaker is saying. Create a mental model of the information being communicated. Whether a literal picture or an arrangement of abstract concepts, your brain will do the necessary work if you stay focused and with your senses fully alert. When listening for long stretches, concentrate on, and remember, key words and phrases. When it's your turn to listen, don't spend the time planning what to say next. You can't rehearse and listen at the same time. Think only about what the other person is saying. Finally, concentrate on what is being said, even if it bores or angers you. If your thoughts start to wander, immediately force yourself to refocus.

Step 6: Try to feel what the speaker is feeling. If you feel sad when the person with whom you are talking expresses sadness, joyful when he or she expresses joy, fearful when he or she describes her fears—and convey those feelings through your facial expressions and words—then your effectiveness as a listener is assured. Empathy is the heart and soul of good listening.

Respond

Step 7: Don't interrupt and don't be a sentence grabber. Don't try to speed the conversation by interrupting and finishing others' sentences. This usually will land you way off base and will impede the conversation, throwing your speaker off track. Just keep listening until the speaker pauses, at which point you can let him or her know you've been listening by saying something like, "Here's what I hear you saying...is that right?" You can also ask for more information or an explanation if you don't understand what the speaker is saying.

Interrupting sends a variety of messages. It says, "I'm more important than you are," "What I have to say is more interesting, accurate, or relevant," "I don't really care what you think," "I don't have time for your opinion," or "This isn't a conversation, it's a contest, and I'm going to win."

If you're trying to connect, you have to be where the other person is—neither above nor below. We all think and speak at different rates. If you are a quick thinker and an agile talker, the burden is on you to relax your pace for the slower, more thoughtful communicator—or for the person who has trouble expressing him- or herself.

Step 8: Give the speaker regular feedback. Show that you understand where the speaker is coming from by reflecting the speaker's feelings with phrases like, "You must be thrilled!" "What a terrible ordeal for you," and "I can see that you are confused." If the speaker's feelings are hidden or unclear, then occasionally paraphrase the content of the message. You can also nod and show your understanding through appropriate facial expressions and an occasional, well-timed "hmmm" or "uh huh."

Step 9: Don't impose your "solutions." When listening to someone talk about a problem, refrain from suggesting solutions. People need you to listen. Somewhere way down the line, if you are absolutely bursting with a brilliant solution, at least get the speaker's permission. Ask, "Would you like to hear my ideas?"

Step 10: Stay on track. At dinner, a friend is telling you about her recent trip to Hawaii and mentions that she took scuba-diving lessons. You jump in with, "I can't believe it! I just saw a movie about scuba diving! It was the other day with Paul. Remember him? By the way, did you hear that he and his wife are getting a divorce?" Just like that, the discussion shifts to Paul. This particular conversational affront happens all the time. Sometimes we work our way back to the original topic, but we often don't. When you notice that your question has led the speaker astray, take responsibility for getting the conversation back on track by saying something like, "It was good to see Paul, but tell me more about your adventure in Hawaii."

Conclude

Step 11: Summarize. At the end of every conversation in which information is exchanged, conclude with a summary statement. In conversations that result in agreements about future obligations or activities, summarizing ensures accurate follow-through and feels perfectly natural.

Relationships

Remembering that change involves everyone around us, we are not alone on our change journeys, whether we like it or not! During the stress of change, sometimes we just want to be left alone to think it all through, to plan, and to remain calm. I do recommend you try to get somewhere quiet or even away from your usual surroundings as part of your change journey. Eventually you'll need to embrace the people in your life—and your system—as part of what is impacted by your change.

We need our systems, our people, to support us through this change. We are humans, not created to survive nor thrive only on our own. It's important that we manage our relationships as part of an effective change program.

Partnership and Moods

Start with understanding the people closest to you and this change situation using empathy, which allows you to see the situation from others' perspectives. How is your change goal and your change journey affecting them practically and emotionally? If your goal is to train for a marathon and you are gone from home four hours a day doing your long runs and cross-training, how does that impact your partner and your children? If your goal is to start your own business, how does it impact the household finances or your travel schedule? Engage those with whom you have close relationships—or share living or working space—early in the process as co-creators of your change. This gives them buy-in and emotional investment, which is important to your support as well as gives them the respect and consideration they deserve as part of your system. Once you have your change defined and your journey outlined, articulate it often and clearly to those closest to you.

We each have our own unique ways of handling stress. Some people become control freaks, micromanaging details of their and others' lives. Others retreat from social contact and can become a bit reclusive, preferring to keep their misery to themselves—or needing their space to figure themselves out. Another common symptom is getting cranky, cold, or impersonal with others. It's common to feel irritable and find others irritating. Even the people we adore and to whom we have pledged our lives can grate on our nerves. All emotions can be heightened during change-related stress. It can help to remember that, as challenging as they can be, relationships also can bring support for you and your change.

Since we are all parts of systems, and all change impacts our entire systems, we can't ignore those closest to us during change. This can be difficult since we're also focusing on managing our goals, actions, resources, and other aspects of our change. I'm a believer in communication as the bridge to understanding and relationship management during change, whether you're the one experiencing change or are in relationship with someone who is.

Begin by building an emotional protective barrier around all of the great things that you and your partner share and shelter him or her against all the minor annoyances that the change is sending your way. Remind yourself of all the wonderful qualities that first drew you to your partner and make an effort to see those qualities even in those moments when he or she is driving you nuts.

Communication

The key to all relationships—and to successful change efforts—is effective communication informed by self-awareness, humility, kindness, and grace. Here are a few basic techniques to remember during this time of change:

1. Practice using "I" statements. Stay true to your feelings without blaming others.

2. State your opinions and feelings clearly and without apology.

3. Accept compliments with grace. Yes, it's possible people will think you're doing a great job with this change!

4. Keep your boundaries clearly drawn so that you can focus on your change journey. Practice saying no, especially when people

delegate inappropriately to you or don't realize that your change situation is putting new demands on you.

5. Ask for what you need. Don't assume people know.

6. Deal with conflict directly and swiftly. Have difficult conversations with courage and confidence, remembering your heightened emotional state.

7. Focus on unhooking emotionally from situations with difficult people. Instead, focus on your reaction. You can't control the behavior of others. You can only control your reaction.

8. Build your self-confidence and stay focused on your value. This gives you the courage to communicate effectively. Make sure you are balancing your communication style so that it is not aggressive or passive-aggressive.

Remember, you might be changing in ways people might not recognize or appreciate. It is your responsibility to communicate authentically about these changes and your reactions to them. An example statement could be the following: "I'm just not myself since (the change) happened. If it's been hard to be around me recently, it's because I'm feeling (disconnected with myself or insert other emotion)." Follow this up with an action statement of what you are doing to manage the change or ask for their help if you need it.

Communicate clearly and assertively about your feelings and what you're going through. Explain the changes you're facing to your partner and how they are affecting your emotions and changing your behaviors. Use "I" statements to clearly express your opinion and build your comfort level with assertive communication over time. (See communication-leadership-change.com for more details about effective communication.)

Finally, even the most self-aware, empathetic person under the stress of change needs a break. When you're about to reach your limit (not after you've blown up), give yourself a time-out. Go for a walk, drink water, practice deep breathing, repeat your mantras, go shopping, call a friend, write in your journal, or do some gardening, for example. You'll come back to the relationship calmer and more ready for the ongoing challenges of relationships and change.

4. BRIDGE TO THE FUTURE

You can never cross the ocean until you have the courage to lose sight of the shore.

- *Christopher Columbus*

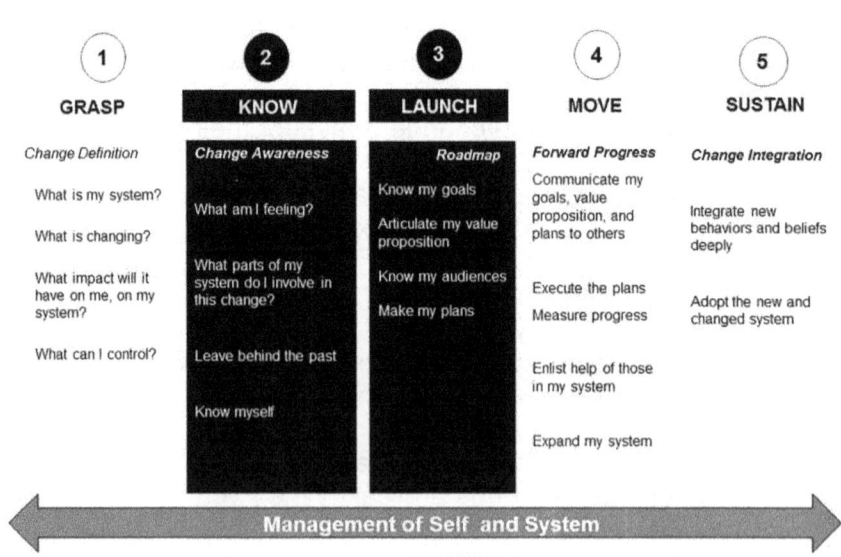

We're moving out of phase 2 of change, where we now have a better understanding of the change situation, ourselves, and others. Phase 3 is where we initiate action toward our change goals. We're not quite there yet. For now, we are in a bridge phase, preparing more deeply to launch.

In trying to move forward with your change, are you feeling weighed down or heavy? Do you feel something is holding you back from freely and lightly stepping out onto your path of change? These could be emotions and memories from your past burdening you and making it difficult for you to move ahead with your journey. In this section, we talk about forgiveness as an important cleansing and lightening concept. We also speak of gratitude as the way to solidify and ground your new clarity. Travel well and travel lightly.

Forgiveness

The key to forgiveness is in not expecting the other to change, to give love, to be kind, and develop the ability to see that in everyone else's eyes and heart there is some good.
—*Francis Bacon*

Sometimes change is caused by a deep transgression, such as infidelity, physical or psychological abuse, unethical behavior, bullying, discriminatory behavior, deception, and lies. What makes these transgressions so dire is that they threaten our core values and morals. This makes them difficult to resolve, and they often involve judgments that lead to a rejection of the behaviors or, sometimes, of the entire relationship.

Whether you are dealing with a deep transgression, or any situation that has hurt you or caused you to doubt yourself, forgiveness is important if you don't want these feelings to impact your future happiness and success.

A lot of us grew up in organized religious structures and belief systems, many of which have a tremendous amount to say about forgiveness, but not all of it resonates as positive. Some of it is fraught with images and rules of punishment and restitution, heaven and hell, revenge, making people pay, suffering consequences, and other scary concepts. I present some thoughts on forgiveness that are absent of any religious or spiritual tendency except that which you choose for yourself. Rather than focusing on forgiveness as a religious obligation, we will be talking about a human response to an emotional reality.

There is a lot of pain in this world, and subsequently, a lot of literature on forgiveness. Putting it together, I have come up with this guide.

Start with reflection about what is keeping you from forgiving this person or group of people. Maybe the reason is one of the following:

• You or the other person do not desire truthfulness.

• You want to protect yourself from further hurt or from the pain of conflict.

• You desire revenge, and forgiving the person will get in the way.

• You are experiencing pressure from friends, family members, or coworkers to not forgive.

• You equate forgiveness with giving in, being subordinate, or not being powerful.

• The offense was very serious.

• You would give up your victim status (and the resulting attention and care from others) if you forgave.

Hosur, Tamilnadu, India

Because forgiveness is empowering and healing and brings you closer to all that is good in you and others, I urge you to find ways to forgive. Forgiveness can help you let a situation go, move on, move forward, and have the future you want.

Start with forgiving yourself. We walk around with anger and pain, and we point at others as the cause. Is our true pain really from them? Or did we do something we consider unforgiveable, and that's the true source of our pain?

Sometimes the hardest person to forgive is yourself. After all, while we understand that we can't control others, we can and should be able to control ourselves, right? We should be able to make great decisions, deal with politics and disappointment with wisdom and benevolence, and call upon our education and skills to have the life we want, right? Not really. Not always. We're humans in an imperfect world dealing with other humans, and they trigger us and impact us.

See yourself as a beautiful human being doing your best to navigate this complex system we call our world. Be as kind to yourself as you would be to your child—gently guiding rather than sternly chastising or harshly berating. This is especially difficult if your standards for yourself are high.

Forgive yourself for any mistakes you've made, for any disappointment you've caused yourself, for the times you didn't live up to your ideas and goals, and for just being too hard on yourself. Forgive yourself, and you can forgive others.

Steps to Forgiveness

Step 1: Acknowledge Your Emotions

Many of us have grown up trying to control our anger and other emotions, judging them as wrong. Emotions are normal human reactions, and they do not disappear just because we deny them. Further, anger is sometimes justified. The trick is to acknowledge and feel the anger as a first step—just don't let it fester and don't wallow in it. Try to recognize what you are angry about. It might be caused by an event that happened months ago.

Step 2: Admit the Loss and Consequences

Look at the true consequences of the event, honestly noting any changes. Were you physically injured? Were you emotionally hurt? Did you suffer financial loss? What other types of losses occurred? Was there harm to other relationships? It helps to record or write down all of these answers, perhaps, in a forgiveness journal.

Step 3: Submit to a Feeling of Vulnerability

This step is harder than it might seem. From youth, we learn to protect ourselves by denying we have any feelings (we're way too cool, too untouchable, or too above it all), much less socially unacceptable emotions like anger. The next stage in forgiveness is to open yourself up to feeling dissonant and awful. Emotions only get stronger and more demanding if ignored. Give them the attention they deserve.

Acknowledge that the feelings of anger in this situation are not working for you, that you don't like them, that you don't want them in your life, and that they are preventing you from being the happy, light, productive, charming person you were meant to be. Also, thank the feelings for teaching you something important, for bringing you closer to yourself, and for letting you see the truth of the situation. Remember that emotions cannot harm you if you let them go. Let them pass through you and out of your life, leaving you free, light, and open to all the good in life.

Step 4: Stop Punishing

A common response to pain is to try to punish those who we believe have harmed us. We do this by harsh and mild methods—withholding companionship, the silent treatment, legal action, spreading negative gossip, property damage, career sabotage, reputation smearing, and other tactics. What does it usually accomplish? You gain an even more solid enemy, and do you feel better? Usually not or at least not for long.

In order to truly forgive, try to let go of the idea that you or the other person should be punished. You can take practical steps to make amends (fixing items, repairing property, paying what you owe, cleaning up, or correcting rumors you or the other person has spread) and ask that the other person join you in that. If they don't, it might mean you can't have a relationship with them anymore. That sometimes is a sad result of painful situations. You can control only your response and your forgiveness. Your task is to try to practice compassion and work at developing a deeper understanding of how and why people behave.

Step 5: Identify Some Good in the Other Person

This step is probably the most crucial in bringing about lasting forgiveness. It can also be the hardest, depending on the severity of the event you are trying to forgive. In forgiving, you try not to think of yourself as being good and the other person as bad. Imagine that each person has goodness in him or her. Finding something good in the person might not be enough to forgive him or her completely. This step loosens your heart a bit, allowing forgiveness to settle in.

Step 6: Let It Go

In the process of resolving negative emotions and thoughts about yourself and the other person, you let go of assuming any debt is owed to you. It is done. Forgiving is not the same as forgetting, however. You do learn the lessons of the situation, and you address the reality that you might have had to spend money to repair something, end a relationship, or otherwise suffer. You don't forget the event and how you felt. It did happen, and now it's part of you and your system forever. Letting it go in forgiveness means you don't hold on to bad feelings, and you don't let them block you from your future. You have achieved this step when, in thinking about the situation, you feel calm and peaceful.

Step 7: Stay in the Present

Letting go means moving on. Stay in the present, leaving behind the past situation in which you were hurt. In the present, be objective about what happened, and try to experience it not as a fresh wound, but as a memory, something that can no longer harm you and a situation over which you now have control. Balance your memory of the event with your memory of the forgiveness work you have done.

Gratitude

Appreciative learning (AI) is an approach of rigorous inquiry led by organization development expert Dr. David Cooperrider.[9] This approach helps people emerge from a cycle of ruminating about their misery so that they can focus on what's going well and what is working as a foundation to improvement.

In AI, instead of focusing on problems to solve, you focus on what's going well. It's a matter of perspective. It does not deny that some things might be wrong or bad. It just doesn't focus on those. You can use your own form of AI as you prepare to leave behind the past and move into your future. I use AI as a springboard into gratitude, which I believe goes a long way toward paving a change path with positivity. Whatever happened to bring you up to this moment, find something to be thankful for and hold it in you as you say "thank you" to the people and the circumstances that brought you to this point.

Remember—this doesn't mean you ignore things that were or are genuinely wrong or that you look the other way when people do things to you or others that go against your ethical or moral standards. Life is full of annoyances and pain, and sometimes things just don't go right. Sometimes you are genuinely, tragically wronged. Do experience your natural response to these situations. Just don't wallow. Don't stay there. Switch to gratitude and peace quickly.

Becoming a Grateful Person

While complaining instills in us a sense of lack, being grateful embeds abundance, safety, and joy deeply into us.

Becoming grateful is a simple matter of switching your thoughts to only those things that make you glad. Simple? Not for most of us. The world comes at us hard and fast, and we usually have reasons to be annoyed, angry, sad, and regretful.

But we can learn. Exercising the muscle of gratitude is simple— you just have to focus and keep doing it over and over until it becomes a normal response. I warn you—it won't feel normal at first. You will feel awkward and uncool. People might think you're being sarcastic, deride you for being a "Pollyanna," or even accuse you of killing their own complaining buzz. Keep at it.

Every time you choose a grateful thought and feeling, you will find your body relaxing and becoming energized at the same time. Start with small, everyday situations and switch your response and thinking. The following are some very simple examples to give you an idea of how to start shifting to a grateful response:

Grateful vs. Negative Responses

You discover you're out of coffee when you blearily stagger to your kitchen in the morning.

Grateful responses:

• This gives me the chance to drink tea, which I know is good for me and also will give me a morning pick-me-up.

• Let me try waking up with a walk around the block and a glass of water instead of coffee this morning.

Construction blocked traffic on the way to an important meeting, and you were late.

Grateful responses:

• I'm glad they're making this road wider—this will make my commute faster in the next few months.

• Being late for the meeting gives me an excuse to take the new person on my team out to lunch so he or she can catch me up.

Your ten-year-old's closet is full of half-eaten snacks that you had to clean up.

Grateful responses:

• This gives me a chance to talk to him or her about responsibility.

• I'm glad I have the time to notice what my child is eating and doing.

Your company gave you and your team twenty-four hours' notice that you were being laid off.

Grateful responses:

- I'm glad we were all informed at the same time—at least we can commiserate and support each other.

- It's the start of something new for all of us.

- This is not about me, and this company is clearly going in a direction that does not mean the best for me. I'm glad to be moving on.

Your boss informed you that your latest performance review was negative, and that is the reason you're the only team member not getting a raise this year.

Grateful responses:

- This gives me the chance to discuss my performance review with my boss. I've had questions for a long time.

- I wonder what the others on my team did better or differently than I did this year. I'll find out by talking to one or two of them.

- I know my boss is usually fair about raises. I'm sure he or she has an explanation that may help me grow.

You discover that your co-committee member has been presenting your ideas as his or hers, getting recognition and great assignments by the chairperson as a result.

Grateful responses:

- This lets me know it's time for me to learn the politics of this organization better and for me to develop skills so I can get what I want here. This coworker is actually someone from whom I can learn.

- I am grateful for this opportunity to look at how I present myself and how others view me. I can use this information to improve my skills at branding myself.

5. MOVING FORWARD

We must be the change we wish to see in the world.

—Mahatma Gandhi

1 GRASP	2 KNOW	3 LAUNCH	4 MOVE	5 SUSTAIN
Change Definition	*Change Awareness*	*Roadmap*	*Forward Progress*	*Change Integration*
What is my system?	What am I feeling?	Know my goals	Communicate my goals, value proposition, and plans to others	Integrate new behaviors and beliefs deeply
What is changing?	What parts of my system do I involve in this change?	Articulate my value proposition		
What impact will it have on me, on my system?		Know my audiences	Execute the plans	Adopt the new and changed system
What can I control?	Leave behind the past	Make my plans	Measure progress	
	Know myself		Enlist help of those in my system	
			Expand my system	

Management of Self and System

Jaya K Bohlmann

We have engaged in phase 1 to understand our change, phase 2 to know ourselves and others, and we have built a solid bridge to phase 3.

Now we initiate. This is when the action starts. In order to create the goals for your change, you need to know what you value and how that differs from what you have.

Value Proposition

You might have heard of value proposition as a tool used for branding companies and products. It articulates what makes them special to customers and others they want to influence. Whether your change is for personal or professional reasons, you can use the value-proposition process to become clear about your desired future state and how it benefits you and others.

First, read the description and examples below. Then you can complete the exercise found at communication-leadership-change.com.

Qualities of an Effective Value Proposition

- Clarity - it's easy to understand.

- It communicates the concrete and tangible results people will get from your product or from hiring, befriending, or being with you.

- It says how you are different or better than other people competing with you.

- It avoids hype, such as "best," "first," and "richest," as well as business jargon.

- It can be read and understood in no more than twenty seconds.

- It includes tangible, valuable results to your audience.

Examples

• I am an award-winning project manager with a strong track record of meeting deadlines on high-impact projects that saved employers $10 million and boosted revenue by $15 million over five years, earning three corporate awards and widespread recognition.

• For people going through professional or personal transitions, I am a credentialed and experienced transformation coach with a strong track record of helping people create unique value propositions, improving networking and interpersonal skills, finding professional opportunities that align with their values and goals, and improving their overall life experience.

Chamonix, France

• I am a strong, healthy nonsmoker who has patience and presence with my children, resulting in a happy, engaged family.

• I am a dedicated daughter who cares for her parents with medical and emotional resources. This brings them greater peace and health and gives me the reward of living my value in this area.

• I am a fit, lean athlete who trains regularly for marathons through cross-training and distance work, keeping my diet protein rich, and keeping my meditative life solid. This allows me to maintain my desired weight, keep my mind focused, and win races!

• I am a strong leader who has brought together colleagues of various professional disciplines to work as a team to achieve corporate goals, growing business typically by a minimum of 30 to 50 percent over the year while cutting costs by 35 percent.

• I am a published technology writer with thousands of social media followers, who report that using my techniques increased their productivity by 61 percent and sales by 30 percent over six months. My content helps people leverage the Internet to triple their market reach and cut marketing costs in half when launching new products.

For organizations in transition, I am a credentialed and experienced corporate communication and behavior coach and executive with a strong track record of leading high-impact initiatives that save millions of dollars, boost revenues, and increase market and mind share due to effective rebranding as well as innovative use of the communication function and growth of its team members.

• For people suffering from illnesses not fully helped by current medical treatments, I offer natural medicine remedies and protocols.

•For organizations with public policy priorities, I am an experienced attorney with corporate and nonprofit expertise, combined with an entrepreneurial approach, superb analytics, and research skills as well as the ability to articulate complex subject matter to the right audiences, inspiring them to act and think in ways important to their goals.

Setting Goals

A man is not old until regrets take the place of dreams.

—John Barrymore

The value proposition tells the world what we have to offer and why they should care. Now you need to know where you are going. The bridge linking passion, vision, and action is paved with goals.

A goal is a one-sentence statement of your desired end-stage—what do you want to accomplish within what time frame? The SMART formula for goal setting (Specific, Measureable, Achievable, Realistic, Time bound) is one of the most widely used goal-setting tools. Working through it can help you develop clear, timely, significant, and attainable objectives. More importantly, this exercise can help you clarify what you really want and help you think through all the steps needed to achieve it.

The online worksheet found at communication-leadership-change.com provides a template for you to set your SMART goals. Here is a guide.

Specific: You clearly state where you are going.

- What exactly do you want to accomplish?

- What will it look like when you reach your goal?

- What exactly will you have accomplished at the end of this process?

- What is the specific outcome you want?

Measurable: You've included a way to see if you are making progress.

- How can you quantify this goal—put it into a number—so that you will know when you've reached it?

- Be specific. Words such as "more," "increase," "improve," "larger," and "better" are too vague. Work to refine definitions so that anyone can understand your goals.

Attainable: It is within your capabilities and depends only on you.

- Is this goal reasonably possible?

- Are there any barriers that could prevent you from reaching your goal?

- If this goal depends on anyone other than you, how can you reword it so that only you are in control?

Relevant: You care enough about this goal to make it a priority.

- Why is this important to you?

- To which other goals does this relate?
- What are you willing to do, sacrifice, or spend to have this goal?
- How important is this goal to you?

Time Bound: What is the deadline for accomplishing the goal and subgoals?

- When will you start?
- When will you achieve interim goals?

Time Management

When I let go of what I am, I become what I might be.

—Lao Tzu

Time-related stress is very common, occurring when your to-do list is unrealistic or unexpected events throw you off track. During change, when you might already be overwhelmed and feeling there is a lot to deal with, it's important to manage your time so that you don't become further stressed.

Good time-management skills include making to-do lists that are realistic, creating action programs, setting reminders for deadlines, creating time limits for various tasks and sticking to them, and staying focused. Even more important than these daily tactics is keeping your true goals in mind and not filling your time with unrelated activities. Further, know your priorities so that when the inevitable interruptions or distractions come along, you are clear about how to spend your time if it becomes limited.

Try this: Make a list of all the things you need and want to get done in a day or week. Then cross off (or postpone) anything not related to your specific change-related goals.

There are probably items on your to-do list you can let go.

For example, if cleaning the entire house on your day off every week is preventing you from having any leisure time, perhaps you can fit a cleaning service into your budget. If ironing shirts is keeping you up late at night, send them to the cleaners instead. If these seem like luxuries you can't afford, try to reorganize your budget a bit. Remember that your time is valuable too.

6. BE YOUR OWN CHANGE

I'm starting with the man in the mirror I'm asking him to change his ways; and no message could have been any clearer - if you want to make the world a better place, take a look at yourself, and then make a change.

—Glen Ballard and Siedah Garrett, sung by Michael Jackson

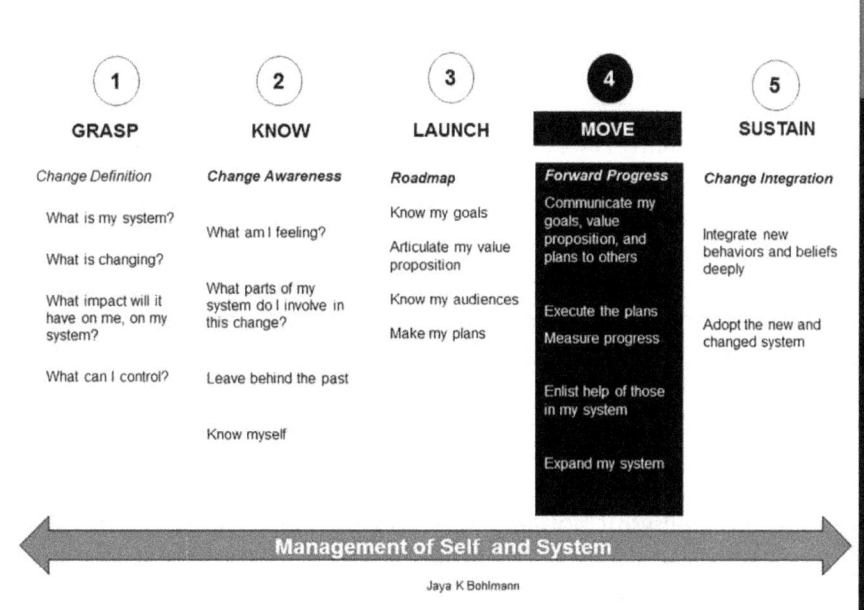

We have completed phase 1, where we came to understand our change, phase 2, where we got to know ourselves and others, and then made our plans to officially launch our change in phase 3. Now in phase 4, we can move with confidence to make our changes come visibly to life. This section describes ways to empower yourself through mental expansion and effective use of your physical and emotional resources

I believe the only real responsibility anyone has on this earth is to be truly, authentically themselves. Why else would we exist? If we are following someone else's ideas, living someone else's values, or tagging along on someone else's dreams, then why be here? Why are we each given unique bodies, minds, and DNA? I think it's so we can make our own unique imprint on all that came before us in history and all that is still to come. We have nine or ten decades to show the world who we are—make it count. You can't make it count if you're in the shadows, trembling with fear, doubt, debt, or anything that is holding you back. Step into the light of your whole being and show the world what you've got.

Now that you have begun the work of knowing your values and passions, setting your goals, and creating your value proposition, you can now deeply integrate your self-knowledge so that you can be fully yourself and create the changes you most want.

Ban the Shoulds

A friend, an accomplished and well-loved musician, wanted to make a midlife career change. With a goal to move to a new city, she began to make plans to leave an established position in the education field and her hometown. She had no firm goals after that, and her family and some friends were puzzled and nervous for her. They expressed this to her in phrases such as, "You should think about a plan B," "You should really plan for retirement," "You shouldn't sell your house yet," "You should have health insurance," and "You should have a stable situation at this point in your life." This last sentence was a very popular one.

She continued with her plans, and today, ten years later, she's had an exciting and rich journey, literally and figuratively. She has lived in New York and several other cities, buying and selling beautiful houses, working in interesting and challenging jobs in music and other industries, and deepening her relationship with herself. While many people would consider her experience productive and exciting—and so does she, for the most part—she still sometimes questions if she should be doing it all differently. Should she focus just on a music career? Should she pursue some career ideas she started but didn't find rewarding (lest she be judged for that too)? Should she sell her house to be more financially prudent? Should she...or shouldn't she?

After talking it through, she decided to ask a different question. Instead of asking, "Should I?" she is asking, "What do I want?" Focusing on the shoulds blocked her from letting her true goals and desires through. Once she let the shoulds go, she was able to stop rebelling against them. Now she is living according to her desires, which are in the musical and artistic areas of her life. She is happier and more fulfilled for it.

The shoulds will kill your dreams faster than a low bank balance, career setbacks, depression, or lack of direction. In fact, those darn shoulds can be powerful enough to bring your whole self to a standstill, with the inertia of self-doubt grinding you to a halt. The question isn't "What should you be doing?" Rather, it's "What do you value?" What do you want to do? What do you feel called to do?

Whose voices are in your shoulds? Most of us are actually hearing our parents, teachers, spouses, and children. Those are important people, for sure, and influential parts of your personal system, but they aren't you. Only you can say what is true for you in terms of action and decision. (That is the power of knowing your passions and your values, as we discussed earlier.)

Here's the test: Next time a should pops into your thoughts ("I should do the laundry," "I should send my résumé to the recruiter today," or "I shouldn't eat the doughnut"), tune in to your feelings. Does the should give you energy, or does it deplete you, leaving you feeling tired, fatigued, sad, and slightly depressed? Here's another test: Replace the word "should" with "want." Is it still true for you? Do you want to do the laundry, send in the résumé, or eat the doughnut? You might not want to now, but you might later. You might not want to do the action, but you might want the reward—as in, you might not want to do the laundry, but you do want clean clothes; you might not want to deprive yourself of the doughnut, but you do want to stay on your diet. If this is the case, you'll need to decide if you can get help doing the task so that you can enjoy the outcome and reward or if you can rally yourself to the task, changing your "should" into a "want."

Sedona Arizona, USA

Remembering, Reframing, Intuition, and Intellect

Go confidently in the direction of your dreams. Live the life you have imagined.

—*Henry David Thoreau*

I have an uncle who, responding to a medical diagnosis at the age of sixty-two, decided to take up marathon running. He had never run long distances before—in fact, he had never regularly exercised. Instead of thinking of himself as sick, old, or physically unfit, he reframed his situation to think of himself as a runner and as someone who could master mind over body, one marathon at a time. His illness was managed and even went into remission for several decades. When, sadly, he recently passed away, he left behind a room full of marathon medals from all over the world, and a world full of admirers. Not only did he reframe his image for himself, he forced the world to see him and his situation differently too.

Regret is debilitating. It creates frustration and pain when people express sadness at no longer being as good as they used to be, when they remember bad things that happened, when they didn't get what they wanted, or when someone let them down. Sometimes, people are even sad when they remember happy times because they wish they were still here.

But we can't do anything about the past except feel bad! If you're holding on to regret about a situation, learn its lesson and move into the future.

There is nothing except the present moment. Your past has caused thoughts, feelings, information, images, and perceptions that are now part of you, but the only thing you can act on is this present moment. Where are you standing right now? What situation, mood, or condition are you in right now?

Reframe your thoughts about the past so that you can do something about them now. If you used to be physically fit and you want to be again, you can take steps now to achieve your health goals. If you used to be rich, you still have what it takes to make money. If you used to have a job you loved, many great opportunities are still waiting for you. If you've never had the things you now want, now is the time to create.

Your first step isn't to scramble around, trying to control circumstances. Instead, look within yourself first. Your future is at the place where your heart, mind, and spirit create your external circumstances.

That isn't to say that we can or should forget our pasts. This is our personal history, rich with lessons from which we can grow. We just can't get stuck in the past, unable to act appropriately in the present. Pain and regret are powerful blocks to progress. Like watching a horror movie, sometimes we get so fascinated by replaying the traumatic scenes from our past because we just can't stop. We may be drawn to the drama, the pain, or the discomfort. Or perhaps we are honestly trying to understand what we're supposed to learn and trying to heal the pain so we can move on.

Adding to what was said earlier about forgiveness, think about this: A way to heal emotional pain and unblock the interfaces in our systems is reframing.

Reframing is part of cognitive therapy, pioneered in the 1960s by University of Pennsylvania psychiatrist Aaron Beck.[10] His theory is that thoughts control feelings. In other words, changing the way that you think about an event changes how you feel about it. In this manner, the outlook a person has on life can be changed from negative to positive simply by changing thought patterns and perceptions.

Cognitive reframing requires that you consciously change a thought or perception as soon as it takes place. It requires that you propose alternative mental scenarios to yourself—different ways of looking at what's happening to you. It takes practice, but if you keep at it, cognitive reframing will start to happen automatically.

When the emotion is gone, your mind is no longer attached to the belief. Suddenly, your mind is free to reprocess it and realize that it isn't true or that there are easy ways around it.

Psychological experts (Og Mandino, Lynn Grabhorn, and others[11]) describe reframing as stopping the focus on negative aspects of our situations and switching to feeling good about anything positive we can find, however small. Focusing on the positive makes us feel better, and only good feelings are creative.

This practice sounds easy, but focusing on the positive aspects requires work for most of us. Mostly, we stay in our intellect and "think" positive while harboring feelings of dread, doubt, anxiety, and sadness. These feelings will actually create what we don't want.

Switching to good feelings requires an internal emotional network of clear channels, which are the places in our minds and bodies that take in emotions, recognize and absorb them, and, sometimes, hold onto them too long. Most of the time, we walk around with blocked or semiblocked internal channels—muddied by troublesome thoughts and negative emotions, memories that make us sad, or dire future predictions that scare us. Our channels can even be blocked by our physical condition and habits, some of which we perform with the intent of unblocking ourselves, but they have the opposite effect. For example, a person may have a cocktail to "take the edge off" a hard day, stay up too late watching movies to escape, or might even do more harmful things.

Rather than clear our channels, these actions usually block us even more.

Seek to cleanse rather than block. Find all the ways you can to stay open so that you can accept happiness. Staying closed might block pain, but only temporarily, and will also block anything that is healing or positive. Find strength and acceptance to deal with pain and stay open to joy.

Staying open allows us to remain closer to ourselves because we're more open to our feelings, which tell us what our truth is. This is known as intuition—that feeling of lightness and rightness that lets us know which path to take in decisions large and small.

Shakti Gawain, author of Living in the Light[12] says it's crucial to have both intuition and intellect working together. Intuition informs intellect on the right path, and intellect makes it happen, carrying the idea forward into the world.

In times of change and choice, our intellect might be all over the place, kicked around by those pesky negative emotions of doubt, fear, and their many cousins. It could be really difficult to clear through those and hear our intuition. Pay attention to emotions; they have important messages. When they crowd out everything else or overwhelm you, I recommend the following:

Be still, breathe through the emotions, identify and name each one, honor each emotion for the message that it is sending you, and file away any lessons or things to pay attention to. Then dismiss each one, as if they were students in your classroom, and the bell has rung. In the empty room, take an even deeper breath and invite your intuition to come in.

Your intuition is your trusted advisor, your confidante, and your wise counselor. Ask your intuition what to do. Listen to the answers. Feel the peace, joy, love, and excitement in you as you realize that this is the truth for you and the path you want to take. Intellect still resting, don't be tempted to wonder how you will do it, what obstacles will come, or any of the logistics. It's not your job to know that at this time. Fully commit to what your intuition is telling you and then your intellect will make it happen.

La Jolla, California, USA

The Physical Requirements of Change

We've discussed mental changes to support our physical changes. Change also requires mental and physical stamina to do all that's required as well as move through the stages with awareness and appropriate action. I compare this with running, which is my preferred sport.

As a new runner, I was challenged to find my pace. I discovered it tired me to go faster than my usual pace, and I was exhausted when I went more slowly. On the days I didn't feel like running, I still tried to go faster to get it over with and to prove my mastery of mind over body. This really fatigued me, and these are the moments when I fell, twisted an ankle, or just felt ill for days. I became more vulnerable when not honoring the pace most natural and healthy for me.

I think it's the same with change. Since change is difficult, we might be tempted to race through it or move too slowly. Either of these paces might cause us to give up or lose hope. My advice is to travel along your change journey at the right pace for you. Not the pace of fear, doubt, resistance, or the desire of others, but at the pace that makes you feel light, easy, in the zone, and free. On your change journey, honor and commit to this pace by writing in deadlines, milestones, and interim goals. These will turn into your action plans.

Physical stamina and pacing are important change-related resources. So, too, are money, time, emotional support, and physical support. These can come from ourselves or others in our systems. Managed effectively, they can help us meet our change goals. Not given their due attention, they can become the excuses we give for not changing, such as "there isn't enough time to exercise," "there's not enough money to move to a new city," "the house isn't big enough to start my own business," or "I can't put in the hours it takes to get the promotion."

Facts don't hold any power on their own. It is our interpretations of those facts that can make them positive, negative, empowering, or blocking. So when thinking through the facts related to your existing money, time, and other resources, remember that you can control them by changing the way you think about them.

The practical matters related to resources should be addressed as part of your action planning—setting your change goals and the steps you'll take within a specified time frame. You don't have to wait until all your resources are perfectly lined up to move ahead with some of the five distinct steps to change. Remember: Conditions don't have to be perfect for you to start on the change journey. Look around at what you have right now and creatively use those resources with courage and determination.

What do you do with those pesky realities? Get creative, opening your heart and mind to options you might never before have considered.

Can't work out to meet your weight loss goal because you need to get your children to school by 7:30 in the morning? Set a loud alarm and wake up at 5:30 a.m. for at least thirty minutes of cardio, yoga, or whatever works for you.

Still can't work out because you have no money for a gym membership? Map out a one-mile route in your neighborhood and run or walk every day. Roll out a yoga mat in your bedroom and practice for twenty minutes every day.

There are all kinds of examples I could give. Take a moment to think about and write down examples from your own situation. You can achieve your change goals if you take them one step at a time. Trying to do too much (or think too much) all at once can overwhelm and panic you. Just keep moving.

In high school, my best friend and I served on the student council as officers and committee chairs. We took our roles very seriously; we were in charge of planning and executing the large student events. We always began with grand visions of lavish affairs that depended on a great many other people, mainly our classmates. These poor teens, busy with other high school tasks of homework, basketball, and other obligations, invariably fell down on the job. (Clearly they did not see, as we did, the life-altering importance of having the perfect skit at the Fall Festival.) Mere days before said events were to occur, with little accomplished, my friend and I, with the dramatic energy only teenage girls can muster, would collapse together and say to each other, "Now just don't panic," in voices full of alarm and hysteria. From that point, we would always figure out how to move ahead with our plans and get them done.

Acknowledge fear and panic first to honor their place in your situation. Then release those emotions. This opens you up to calm down and move ahead.

7. UNDERSTANDING AND MANAGING THE STRESS OF CHANGE

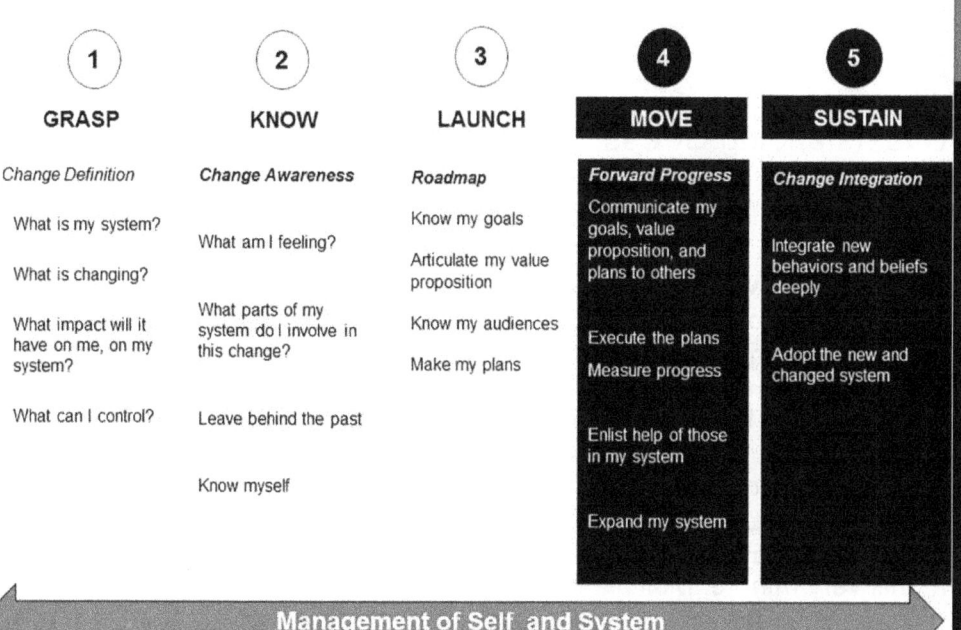

We have now gone through phase 1 to grasp our change situation, phase 2 to gain understanding, phase 3 to launch our change plans, and phase 4 to move into our change more deeply. We are ready to sustain our behaviors, feelings, bodies, and minds so that the change is embedded and integrated into our lives. We are on the brink of our brilliant new normal.

This book is all about change, and even though I want you to focus on its positive impacts, the process is stressful! This chapter provides a basic guide to help you manage the stress of change.

Understanding Stress

Stress has a bad reputation because it is usually considered harmful to us. However, any change, even a positive one, impacts our physiological system. Positive stress—called "eustress"—encompasses events that could be described as happy, such as getting married, buying a new house, welcoming a newborn child, or starting a new and welcomed job. We usually don't worry about eustress as a negative condition. In fact, we enjoy it and all the good feelings that come with it.

Stress becomes negative if we face continuous challenges without relief, leading to *distress*, which is what we usually think of when discussing stress. A common condition of modern life, distress is affecting most of us at this very minute. Multiple studies agree.

In a 2014 study about stress in America, almost half of all respondents (49 percent) reported that they had experienced a major stressful event or experience in the past year.[13] Close to three-fourths of those polled identified their health as a sphere affected by stress. The most commonly reported effect on health was poor emotional well-being (63 percent), followed by problems with sleep (56 percent), and difficulty thinking, concentrating, or making decisions (52 percent). Other studies tell us that most (75 percent to 90 percent) doctor's office visits are for stress-related ailments and complaints.

Stress can play a part in problems such as headaches, high blood pressure, heart problems, diabetes, skin conditions, asthma, arthritis, depression, and anxiety. Clearly, we must manage our stress.

Effects of negative stress...		
...On the body	...On the mind	...On behavior
• Muscle tension or pain • Chest pain • Fatigue • Change in sex drive • Upset stomach • Trouble sleeping	• Anxiety • Restlessness • Lack of motivation or focus • Irritability or anger • Sadness or depression	• Changed eating behaviors • Mood swings • Substance abuse • Social withdrawal

Types of Stress

We all deal with multiple stressors every day. Each needs to be managed appropriately, beginning with understanding them. Dr. Karl Albrecht, a pioneer in the development of stress-reduction training, defined four common types of stress in his 1979 book *Stress and the Manager*.[14]

1. Time stress—worrying about not having enough time to do the number of things that you have to do, and you fear that you'll fail to achieve something important. You might feel trapped, unhappy, or even hopeless. Common examples: worrying about deadlines or rushing to avoid being late for a meeting.

2. Anticipatory stress—worrying about the future. Sometimes this stress can be focused on a specific event, such as an upcoming presentation. However, anticipatory stress can also be vague and undefined, such as an overall sense of dread about the future or a worry that "something will go wrong." Common situations include taking a test, or speaking in public.

3. Situational stress—feeling scared in a situation over which you

have no control.

> Some common examples: Getting laid off or making a major mistake in front of your team or family.

4. Encounter stress—worrying about interacting with a certain person or group of people. You might not like them or you might think that they're unpredictable. Encounter stress can also occur if your role involves a lot of personal interaction with customers or clients, especially if those groups are in distress. Common examples: Physicians and social workers have high rates of encounter stress because the people they work with routinely don't feel well or are deeply upset. This type of stress also occurs from "contact overload"—when you feel overwhelmed or drained from interacting with too many people.

All of these types of stress are present every day. During change, they can feel more intense because of the potential for you to feel more vulnerable and unsure.

When to Seek Help

The techniques mentioned in this book provide basic information and guidance to help you manage and overcome stress. It is not intended as official medical advice—this can only come from your physician. Please talk to your doctor about your specific health issues related to stress or other conditions. Further, if you've taken steps to control your stress but continue to have troubling or uncomfortable symptoms and find it difficult to work, rest, or perform daily activities, see your doctor.

Stress and Your Body

Experts say our inherent fight-or-flight response was created for a more primitive time, when our ancestors regularly had to hunt and kill for food and to ward off predators that were daily threats. In those situations, the body responds as follows: Digestion stops, reproductive

Digestion stops, reproductive organs are not as active, and adrenal glands get busy pumping out hormones that cause epinephrine (adrenalin)to course through our veins.

This increases the heart rate dramatically and constricts our arteries to increase the speed at which nutrients in the blood reach tissues, including muscles. All of this empowers us to react quickly to the threats.

Today, rather than fighting with hungry beasts, we seethe with impatience at the slow checkout line at the store, race toward a work deadline, yell at drivers in stop and go traffic on congested roads, or tense up at an angry confrontation with our boss. Our bodies perceive these situations in the same manner. That's why our hearts pound as we approach the boss's office, our palms sweat as we walk up to the front of the room to deliver the presentation, and our legs tremble and twitch as we anxiously wait for the traffic light to switch to green.

This physiological response works well as designed—the threat is responded to, then disappears, and our systems calm down. The negative physical impact of stress occurs when we are stressed for long periods of time, and we don't reach the calming-down stage. During times of change, all of these effects could be heightened. This makes it even more important that we understand what's happening to our bodies and how to mitigate the negative impact of stress.

In 1936, Hans Selye, who is called the "father of stress," was the first to give a scientific explanation for biological "stress."[15] He borrowed the term "stress" from physics to describe an organism's physiological response to perceived stressful events in the environment. Selye created the stress model General Adaptation Syndrome (GAS), based on physiology and psychobiology. The model states that an event that threatens an organism's well-being—a stressor—leads to a three-stage bodily response.

Stages of General Adaptation Syndrome (GAS)

ALARM ▶ **RESISTANCE** ▶ **EXHAUSTION**

| Once a stressor is perceived, the body goes into the fight-or-flight response, and the sympathetic nervous system is activated so that the body is mobilized to meet the threat. | In an effort to compensate, the parasympathetic nervous system attempts to return many physiological functions to normal levels. Meanwhile, the body remains on alert. | If the stressor continues beyond the body's capacity, the body's resources become exhausted, and the body becomes susceptible to disease and death. |

The intensity of the stress response is governed largely by glucocorticoids, the primary molecules involved in the stress response. Chronic exposure to these hormones causes physical symptoms, including headaches, upset stomach, elevated blood pressure, chest pain, skin issues (hives, eczema, dermatitis, and psoriasis), aches and pains, hair loss, diminished sex drive, and problems sleeping. Research suggests that stress can also bring on or worsen certain symptoms or diseases, including the following:

- Heart disease and high blood pressure. Most cardiac care programs incorporate stress management and exercise, and stress reduction

- Weakened immune system. Certain molecules, particularly cortisol, suppress the immune system and inflammatory pathways, rendering the body more susceptible to disease. This, in turn, can cause a variety of responses, such as prolonged healing times, inability to cope with vaccinations, heightened vulnerability to viral infection, impaired cognition, decreased thyroid function, and the accumulation of abdominal fat.

Stress is unavoidable. Long-term stress is too harmful to ignore. Since your change journey might be a long one, it makes sense to manage your stress by understanding and altering your behaviors, thoughts, feelings, and physical responses.

Reducing the strength of your stressors is usually a more viable option than eliminating them entirely. There are several techniques for learning to stay calm and clearheaded under pressure. As you master them, even your biggest stressors will pose less of a threat.

Managing Stress

Just Breathe

Stress tends to cause our breathing to become shallow and rapid. When the stress is gone, we inhale into the depths of the diaphragm and exhale fully. Breathing deeply into your abdomen and lower back signals the parasympathetic system to allow you to relax. Practicing deep and full-belly breathing can fool your body into thinking it is relaxed even when you're stressed. Do this when faced with a challenging situation, such as just before an interview or a public speaking engagement. It is also a very good way to calm yourself just before sleeping at night.

To condition your breathing muscles, practice every day to instill deep breathing as a habit. Take at least ten full-belly breaths in and exhale completely. This also will instill deep breathing as a habit.

> **7-11 Breathing Technique**
>
> 1. Inhale for seven counts.
> 2. Hold briefly.
> 3. Exhale for eleven counts.
> 4. Repeat.
> 5. Visualize positive thoughts upon exhalation.

Just Move

Exercise is one of the most important things you can do to mitigate the poor effects of stress. Many experts have studied the connection between exercise and the brain, and they say that exercise is truly our best defense against everything from depression to addiction.[16] Exercise has been shown to work better than antianxiety medication for relaxing the mind and body during times of stress. The proper exercise has the potential to increase blood flow and improve oxygen supply to the tissues.

Exercise can be categorized by the amount of stress it puts on your body, ranging from zero (no stress) to five (highest level). Zero equals sitting on the couch. In an already stressed body, don't add more by over-exercising. Many people I know (including myself) push themselves in hard workouts, thinking this relieves their work or emotional stress. It may help to clear your mind, but it takes a toll on your body that might steadily weaken you, making you susceptible to illness and injury.

In times of high stress, if your usual routine is a four-mile run, walking would be a change from level 5 to a level 2 or 3 exercise intensity, producing gentler and better stress relief. This is not a subpar exercise; although it seems almost too simple, the act of walking has many health and fitness benefits. In addition to the cardiovascular and muscle-toning effects, swinging your arms in sync with your leg stride requires a perfect balancing of impulses from the two halves of the brain and cerebellum; the balance can help you think more clearly.

EXERCISES BY LEVELS: EXAMPLES						
Levels	0	1	2	3	4	5
	Sitting in front of TV, desk or computer	Restorative sleep	Tai Chi	Yoga	Jogging (more than 1 mile)	Distance running
		Deep breathing	Short, easy stroll	Cayce morning exercises (see this chapter)	Body resistance weight training (push-ups, pull-ups, burpees, knee lifts)	Heavy weight training
				Brisk long walk		Kickboxing
				Trampoline bouncing (simple)		Martial arts
				Light resistance training		
				Bicycling (easy)		

When you do the proper level of exercise for you, you will feel better almost every time. If you find yourself running low on energy during your exercise or feeling sore afterward, you have a surefire signal that you need to bring the level down a notch. If you don't feel energized or better mentally after a low level of intensity, try taking it up a notch and see how you feel.

Whether you're a fitness buff or just getting started, we recommend a series of exercises provided by Edgar Cayce, who is often called "the father of holistic medicine."[17] There is a routine for morning and one for evening. An easy to follow description of this routine begins on the following page.

Morning Vertical Setting-Up Exercises

Used with permission and courtesy of Peter Van Daam and the Association for Research and Enlightenment

To be done upon waking after drinking a glass of warm water.

While performing the exercises, be mindful of the exercise itself and pay attention to the movement of the body as described in each exercise. Breathing is meant to be done deeply in through nostrils and out completely through the mouth. Continue deep breathing this way throughout the routine.

Begin with a mantra, a phrase or thought that inspires and energizes you.

Try to reach a maximum of ten to twelve repetitions of each exercise (in each direction.)

1. Deep breathing—Inhale through the nostrils and exhale through the mouth.

2. Twist—Feet apart. Gently twist trunk, shoulders, head, and eyes back and forth, swinging arms with flowing Tai Chi-like movement. Inhale one way; exhale the other.

3. Tilt—Arms rigid, extended sideways, always in line with the shoulders. Tilt side to side.

4. Forward and Back—Inhale and lean forward gently; stretch arms toward the horizon while exhaling. Inhale again as you return to the erect position. Bend back, gently arching the upper back and clasping the hands together behind the back. Pull the elbows together

5. Shoulder Rotation—Rotate shoulders in exaggerated circles, rubbing arms against the torso, inhaling while raising shoulders, and exhaling as the elbows rotate downward. Reverse direction.and exhale.

6. Arm Rotation—Arms at sides. Keep elbows straight and always keep the thumbs pointing down so that the humerus (upper arm bone) is in the best alignment with shoulder socket. Reverse direction, then repeat both directions with the opposite arm.

7. Leg Rotation—Stand on one leg. Turn the toe of the lifted leg inward and maintain this position throughout exercise to isolate the movement of the hip socket. Rotate the leg in small circles with the knees slightly bent. Reverse direction.

8. Jangle—Jog in place on your toes, shaking your arms and hands loosely throughout. Reach to sky, inhaling deeply, with the arms and hands still shaking. Exhale as you lower the arms. *Perform just three repetitions.*

9. Knee Bends on Toes—Hands on hips (or thighs) with the back erect. Exhale as you squat; inhale upon rising.

10. Hip Rotation—Hands on hips. Rotate the hips in exaggerated circles with the knees slightly bent, keeping the head and shoulders relatively stationary. Reverse direction.

11. Hip Rotation in Push-Up Position—Assume a push-up position either on your forearms or hands, with heels of the feet pressed against a wall or stair. Rotate the hips in an exaggerated circle. Reverse direction. Note: This exercise is a bonus exercise and can be added to further strengthen the hips and core.

12. One-Legged Jangle—Place the right hand on the left thigh for support. Stretch the left arm forward and the right leg backward, allowing your body to bend forward. Vigorously shake the imaginary glove and shoe off of the extended hand and foot. Reverse sides. *Perform just three repetitions.*

13. Touching Toes—Feet apart. Inhale deeply, rising on the toes and stretching your hands to the sky, with the upper back gently arched. Hold briefly. Bend forward, reach toward the toes, with the knees unlocked, and exhale. With practice, one can stay on the toes.

14. Jangle—Perform just three repetitions.

15. Flat-Footed Squat—Keep feet shoulder-width apart and always flat. Keep the arms always extended straight ahead. Inhale fully. Exhale as you squat, with your back erect, to as deep a place as possible without undue pain, keeping the arms extended at shoulder height. Inhale as you rise.

16. Crossover—Keep feet apart, with knees unlocked. Inhale while rising on the toes and raising the left hand to sky. Exhale completely as you bend forward with left hand, reaching to grasp the left heel. Repeat the sequence but with the left hand reaching the right heel. Reverse the sequence with the right hand; first bend to touch the right heel and then bend to the left heel. *Perform just three repetitions.*

17. Spleen-Liver Press—Keep legs wide apart. Inhale. Exhale as you compress the left (spleen) side of abdomen against left thigh. Inhale again and then exhale, compressing the right (liver) side of the abdomen against the right thigh. Do three to six repetitions

18. Jangle—*Perform just three repetitions.*

19. Head and Neck—Drop your head gently toward the chest three times. Reverse by raising your chin to the sky three times. Tilt toward one shoulder (with face forward) three times and then to the opposite shoulder. Drop your head to the chest and rotate three times clockwise, then three times counterclockwise. Keep the shoulders stationary and relaxed throughout the exercise. Be mindful of the movement at all times so as not to allow the head to just flop in the direction. Always stay in control of the movement of the head.

20. Alternate Breathing—Close left nostril with the left forefinger. Breathe in deeply while rising to the toes and reaching the right arm to the sky. Imagine that you are bringing strength into the body. Hold briefly and exhale sharply as you bend forward to reach your hand toward the toes. Repeat three to six times on the same side. Reverse the sequence with the right forefinger closing the right nostril. Breathe in deeply while rising to the toes and reaching the left arm to the sky. Imagine that you are bringing balance to the body. Hold briefly and exhale sharply as you bend forward to reach your hand toward the toes. Repeat the same number of times as the first side.

A video demonstration can be found at communication-leadership-change.com.

> Caution: I must remind you that the information provided in this book is not intended to replace the care and advice of your physician. Please check with your doctor before you try any of the exercises or techniques listed above, especially if you are experiencing any abnormal symptoms or have any conditions related to pregnancy, the heart, diabetes, cancer, or another illness.

Get Outside

Research shows that the average American spends about 87 percent of his or her time in enclosed buildings and 6 percent of his or her time in enclosed vehicles. That's a total of 93 percent of your life spent inside.[18]

There are a number of reasons why this is unhealthy for body, mind, and spirit. One reason is that levels of many pollutants concentrate indoors, where levels are often two to five times higher than typical outdoor concentrations.

The natural world has long been associated with health and described as a therapeutic landscape, and a growing body of research demonstrates the benefits of interacting with nature for mental and physical health. However, concern is growing that all of us, especially children, have lost connection to nature, and spend less time being active and outdoors despite the known health benefits of doing so. We watch TV, play computer games, read books, surf the Internet, do housework, and do homework—all inside. At the same time, we're now seeing record rates of obesity worldwide, alarming rates of type 2 diabetes, asthma, Vitamin D deficiency, and attention deficit disorders—all of which may be tied to children spending less time in nature engaged in outdoor activity.

I recommend following experts' advice and getting outdoors every day, even if temperatures are low. Here are some of the benefits:

1. Boost to Creativity and Focus: Walking outside can increase creativity by up to 80 percent. Spending time in nature can lead to improvements in focus.

2. Improve Mood and Self-Esteem: Physical activity or just being outdoors for even five minutes leads to measurable improvements in mood and self-esteem. Outdoor light exposure may help your mood even if it's cold and cloudy. Putting your bare feet on the ground (that soft grass can feel great!) helps to discharge some excess energy from sitting in front of electronics.

3. Increase Vitamin D Levels: It's estimated that 85 percent of the American public is deficient in this important vitamin, which could prevent or reduce the incidence of chronic diseases, including the incidence of several types of cancer.[19] Vitamin D also is necessary to fight infections, including colds and the flu, as it bolsters your immune system to attack and destroy bacteria and viruses. Vitamin D can act as a hormone to promote good gene transcription for healthy cell replication; it also helps to balance calcium in the body.

Researchers have noted that Vitamin D deficiency is prevalent in adults who have increased skin pigmentation (such as those with ancestors from Africa, the Middle East, or India), who always wear sun protection, or who limit their outdoor activities.

Experts agree that appropriate sun exposure is the best way to optimize your Vitamin D levels, and the more time you spend outdoors, the easier it will be for you to naturally keep your levels in the therapeutically beneficial range of fifty to seventy ng/ml (nanograms per milliliter).

4. Healing Potential: Exposure to natural light is inherently healing. One study found that people exposed to 46 percent more sunlight after surgery used 22 percent less pain medication per hour.[20] Research shows that older adults who spend more time outdoors have less pain, sleep better, and have less functional decline, as shown in their ability to carry out their daily activities.

5. Grounding: There's a constant flow of energy between your body and the earth. When you put your bare feet on the ground, you absorb large amounts of negative electrons through the soles of your feet, which can serve as a powerful and abundant supply of antioxidants. So take off your shoes and spend some time walking barefoot in the grass, sand, or mud.

This simple process of "grounding" or "earthing" has been shown to relieve pain, reduce inflammation, improve sleep, enhance well-being, and much, much more.[21]

If you live in an apartment or don't have much outdoor space, remember that even a patio, rooftop, or terrace planter garden can provide benefits. You also can spend time in neighborhood parks. I love to run outside in the warm weather. The sun and breezes refresh me and heal me, and my muscles get a different workout than when I run indoors on the treadmill.

Here are some additional ideas to bring the outdoors into your daily life:

- Walk or bicycle to and from work.

- Walk your child to and from school.

- Take an afternoon walk (if you have children, do this after school so they can participate too).

- Walk your pet daily.

- Do your reading on a park bench or in your yard.

- Spend five minutes outside immediately upon waking.

- Schedule daily outings to parks or playgrounds.

- Make winter sports a weekly occurrence (skiing, ice skating, sledding, or snowshoeing).

If getting outside is difficult for you, you can simply open your windows to let fresh air into your home and office. Ideally, open two windows on opposite sides of the house for cross-ventilation. Keep them open for at least ten minutes, as that will exchange most of the air. Do this during in the warmest part of the day if it is cold outside.

The Power of Sleep

We are meant to sleep about eight hours every night in order to keep our body rhythms in sync with the cycle of the sun.[22] To ensure that you get the sleep you need, try the following sleep hygiene routine:

1. Maintain a regular bedtime, one that allows you to get a full eight hours of rest.

2. Light is a signal to awaken and stay awake. Computers, phones, and tablets beam unnatural light and electromagnetic stimulation into our bodies and keep us awake. Turn off all screens and bright lights at least fifteen minutes before your bedtime. Keep your electronics out of the bedroom or at least away from your bed.

3. Track your use of stimulants. It's not uncommon to fall into the trap of awakening tired and grabbing a few cups of coffee to get going in the morning. This habit causes a lot of stress to the cortisol balance in the body. Replace the coffee with sleep and a balanced, high-protein breakfast.

4. Avoid regular use of chemical sleep or waking aids.

5. Try taking a walk or some other light exercise after your evening meal.

Adaptogens

Many natural remedies for stress relief are readily available at health-food stores and drugstores. It's important to know which ones are the most effective for you. Check with your physician, especially your naturopath. One group of herbal ingredients we recommend is called adaptogens. These are a unique group of herbal ingredients used to improve the health of your adrenal system, which is in charge of managing your body's hormonal response to stress.

Adaptogens have been used in Chinese and Indian Ayurvedic medicine for centuries to boost energy and resilience, especially during stress. Many modern studies show that adaptogens offer positive benefits and are safe for long-term use.[23]

Adaptogens help strengthen the body's response to stress and enhance its ability to cope with anxiety and fight fatigue slowly and gently, without jolts or crashes you might experience if you use stimulants. They have the unique ability to "adapt" their function according to your body's specific needs. Though the effects may be subtle and take time for you to feel them, they are proven to be effective.

Adaptogens work a bit like a thermostat. When the thermostat senses that the room temperature is too high, it brings the temperature down; when the temperature is too low, it brings it up. Adaptogens can calm you down and boost your energy at the same time without overstimulating. By supporting adrenal function, they counteract the adverse effects of stress. They enable the body's cells to access more energy, help cells eliminate toxic byproducts of the metabolic process, and help the body utilize oxygen more efficiently.

Consult a physician trained and experienced in natural medicine to help you decide if adaptogens can help you, and, if so, which ones to take. Some of the popular ones widely available include Asian Ginseng, Eleuthero, Ashwaghanda, and Rhodiola Rosea. Again, check with your naturopath before starting any health program.

Eating for Stress Management

We've all been there. After the pressure-filled meeting, we devour corned beef and pastries from the catering tray. Or down a glass or two of wine at happy hour with friends to wind down.

Or, during an all-nighter studying for exams, we eat a whole package of cookies, half a pizza, and a liter of soda. Stress eating and stress-related weight gain are real problems! Since we don't usually crave carrots and celery when we're stressed, our bodies can suffer tremendously during chan ge, unless we are vigilant about our diet.

When stressed, cortisol levels are high, and we feel anxious—heart racing, uneven breathing, and sweaty palms. This feeling is uncomfortable, so we want the anxiety to go away and take action on our own behalf. Reaching for, preparing, and eating food is an activity that distracts us from our anxious situation and thoughts, which actually does lower cortisol levels and calms us. Often, it's not the food itself that's calming us; rather, it is the activity.

Once you've eaten, your body will normally come out of the sympathetic (fight-or-flight) mode and into parasympathetic (rest-and-digest) mode. This makes you feel calmer. However, watch what you eat. Poor food choices during times of stress have the ability to cause issues with the whole endocrine system as it struggles to understand what to do with the excess fast-burn energy in cakes, cookies, crackers, and cereals.

Some physical effects of a poor diet include the inability to think clearly or concentrate after eating; lethargy and/or sleepiness shortly after eating; and weight gain, generally in the midsection.

Manage your diet for optimal health during the stress of change by following this general advice:

- Many times, thirst is disguised as hunger. When you're under stress and feel hungry, try starting with a whole glass of water.

- Eat a balanced, mostly natural diet. Find some simple meals and snacks that are mostly natural, unprocessed, fiber-rich whole foods. Create a weekly meal plan, then follow it each day. Make each meal high in protein and good fats, which are naturally relaxing. Some suggestions include a handful of soaked raw nuts, a spoonful of natural nut butter, celery and carrot sticks with hummus for protein, avocado slices, and a hard-boiled egg.

- Meditate and reflect about your diet. Ask your body what it really wants to nourish your physical being and your soul. This will help you override your cravings.

- Be very strict about when you eat. Eating at regular intervals helps regulate blood sugar and minimizes cravings.

- Eat slowly and mindfully. Eating fast adds stress to the digestion process. The body must break the food down, which requires high-quality food and time to chew and mix the food with saliva before swallowing.

- Eat enough during mealtime. You should not be hungry a couple of hours after eating, and you should not be sleepy soon after eating. If you are, your body is struggling to keep food stores properly available.

- Reduce caffeine intake. Consuming caffeine too late in the day can affect sleep quality, which impacts stress levels. Too much caffeine in general can make you more emotionally reactive to stress. Learn how much is too much for you.

- Try switching to tea. Drinking caffeinated black, green, or oolong tea varieties may elicit a more alert state of mind, says a 2013 study in *The Journal of Nutrition*.[24] Researchers say that theanine—an amino acid present in these tea varieties—may work synergistically with caffeine to improve attention and focus.

- Drink alcohol in moderation. One glass of red wine at the end of the day can bring relaxation, but too much alcohol can make you restless, elevate sugar levels, cause you to make poor food choices, and lead to many other difficulties.

- Satisfy a carb craving. Eating carbohydrates can stimulate the release of serotonin, your feel-good brain chemical. A 2009 study in *JAMA Internal Medicine*[25] found that adults on a high-carb, low-fat diet were happier over the long term than those on a low-carb diet. Opt for whole grains, such as quinoa and oatmeal, which deliver more fiber and nutrients than refined ones.

- Nibble on chocolate. Recent research, including a study published in 2010 in *JAMA Internal Medicine*,[26] shows that eating dark chocolate can help reduce levels of hormones associated with stress, such as cortisol.

- Exercise lightly after eating. Try taking a relaxing walk, doing breathing exercises, or performing some light stretching.

Most importantly, try to reach for food only when you are truly hungry and eat for nutrition only. Don't eat to calm down. When you are feeling anxious, try a different activity—not eating—to calm down.

Laugh It Off

During change, stay connected to your network of friends and family—people who know you and support you. They can offer advice, serve as a sounding board, and distract you from getting too self-involved, sad, or depressed. Try to make contact with at least one person from your support network every day.

Remember to have fun. A good sense of humor can't cure all ailments, but when you start to laugh, it lightens you mentally and induces physical changes in your body. Laughter can help lessen your depression and anxiety and make you feel happier.

By stimulating circulation and aiding muscle relaxation,

laughter helps reduce some of the physical symptoms of stress. Laughter enhances your intake of oxygen-rich air; stimulates your heart, lungs, and muscles; and increases the endorphins that are released by your brain. A hearty laugh increases and then relaxes your stress response and increases your heart rate and blood pressure.

Over the long haul, laughter could improve your immune system. Positive thoughts release neuropeptides, which help fight stress and potentially serious illnesses. Laughter could also relieve pain by causing the body to produce its own natural painkillers.

Some of my favorite laugh-inspiring activities can be found on communication-leadership-change.com. What are yours?

Mind Over Matter

The mind and body are one being and one system. If your body is well balanced, your mind will also be in balance. In addition to exercise, relaxation, and a healthy diet, meditation has been shown to help reverse the negative effects of stress by increasing the number of infection-fighting T cells and feel-good endorphins in your body.[27]

Ironically, when many things are happening at once and your entire system is being disrupted, sitting still to think about nothing can seem like the most impossible and unproductive task. I encourage you to get past that mental block and begin exercising your meditation muscles. As with any activity, it takes consistent practice, patience, and time to get comfortable with it and to see results.

Meditation will help you develop focus and the ability to concentrate on what's happening right now, even while you're consumed with your future. It can help you focus so you can create that desired future, plot your change journey, and process the emotions of change. To make it a deliberate part of your healthy change process, here are some guidelines:

- **Environment**: Create a special place for this practice where you can be alone and uninterrupted. It might be a sunny room where you work or create your change plans. It might be a cozy basement room lit with candles. You might like to have artwork, objects, or plants nearby so these objects of meaning can add solace to your space.

- **Silence:** This is the most healing for meditation. To begin, you might want some meditation music or sounds, but as you gain experience in your practice, move toward silence. In that, our true inner experience will come to awareness, speaking to us in wisdom only known to us. From silence, we can gain stability and calm, as well as the practice of resting in the moment, all on our own. There is steadiness and calmness that comes from sitting in silence. In time, outer and inner silence meet, and you come to rest in the moment.

- **Timing**: If you're new to meditation, start with ten minutes of sitting. As you are ready, extend to 30 minutes, never forcing yourself. Do what feels right for you.

- **Posture**: Whether you sit on a chair or cross-legged on the floor, make sure that your spine is upright, imagining that the top of your head is reaching up to touch the sky. This helps keep your mind from drifting.

- **Eyes**: Keeping your eyes open, lower them and soften your gaze. Closed eyes can make it more difficult to focus your thoughts.

- **Focus**: Meditation has been described as a way of waking up to our lives, referring to our everyday movements, during which we are often preoccupied and not present. Have you ever arrived at your office or home without remembering the drive? Meditation can soften the edgy mind and focus whatever we place at the center of our awareness in soft attention.

- **Breath:** In meditation, begin by paying attention to the breath as a great way to anchor yourself in the present moment. Notice your breath streaming in and out. There's no need to control the breath—just let it be natural. Try counting your breaths to help you settle in to meditation. On your outbreath, silently count up to four. Then return to one. Whenever you notice your thoughts have strayed far away or you find yourself counting to thirty-three, for example, simply return to one. In this way, one is like coming home to the present moment.

- **Thoughts**: As thoughts persist in breaking through, gently let them go by returning focus to the breath. Don't try to stop thoughts; this will just make you feel agitated. Imagine that they are unwelcome visitors at your door—acknowledge their presence and politely ask them to leave. Then shine the soft light of your attention on your breath.

    Acknowledging your thoughts can also encourage creative solutions, which is part of the goal in meditation. At the very least, it highlights your mental fixations so that you can more effectively address them.

- **Emotions**: It's difficult to settle into meditation if you are struggling with strong emotions, such as those that cause feelings of tension or agitation in the body and mind. In meditation, focus on where your body might be reacting. Anger might be a hot feeling in your belly; fear a tight band around your chest; sadness a heaviness in your lower body; or worry a knot between your eyes. Breathe through any of these feelings, first noticing and honoring them for the messages they bring to awareness.

As your thoughts and stories related to these feelings crowd your mind in meditation, continually return to focus on the body.

- **Sounds**: Some like to focus their minds with a hum or the sound "om." I like to find a mantra, a phrase that resonates with me emotionally and physically, positively charging me and calming me while centering me on the particular mood or need of the moment.

In Chapter 8, I've included some change mantras I've found helpful. (For more, go to communication-leadership-change.com.)

Record Your Journey

I've kept a journal since I was very young, recording the daily activities of young girlhood, teen angst, adult drama, sometimes trauma, plans, strategies—the poetry of my life as it rolled along with people coming and going and acting on my stage. The act of getting it out of me and into my precious leather-bound, gold-edged volumes freed me
from the intensity of my feelings, and I could, after finishing my last entry for the day and fastening the tiny padlock, breathe more easily. My mind was then more open to finding solutions, gaining gladness, and looking ahead with hope.

I realized the power and release of seeing intimate feelings in writing that had seemed overwhelming or insurmountable while they were bottled up in my mind. Sharing them with my journal was like sharing with a trusted friend. It lines up the feelings and gives them order, immediately dismissing or diminishing those not as true to me or important and getting me closer to the ones most meaningful.

Research has shown the tremendous benefits of journal writing on our physical and mental health.[28] Writing not only relieves stress and improves mood, but it also boosts the immune system, which helps the body withstand the effects of further stress.

The traditional journal has evolved to the blog, the social media post, the audio note, or the video on Instagram. Those can work too, but remember privacy and confidentiality issues if you choose a public platform like social media. The idea is to get all the chatter out of your head and onto some other medium. As you record, don't judge whether your feelings are appropriate or whether you're producing a good piece—this is just for you.

If you feel a need for even more privacy, you can always delete or destroy the written piece later. Or instead of writing, just talk through your thoughts and feelings with a trusted confidante or out loud to yourself.

Hosur, Tamilnadu, India

A Change-Friendly Environment

We can easily forgive a child who is afraid of the dark; the real tragedy of life is when men are afraid of the light.

—Plato

Now we really get moving to bring our change to life. This step on the change journey is so powerful because it unlocks creative mental energy and gets your physical momentum going. In this section, we discuss creating the best environment for change.

When you walk into your office, what do you notice first? The bright painting of the ocean above your desk? The stack of folders near your computer? The jumble of unopened mail in a corner? The tangle of electric cords blocking your safe path? How do you feel as you notice these items? It might not immediately obvious, however, your environment impacts your thoughts, feelings, emotions, and physical and mental health.[29]

Whether your office, your kitchen, your workout room, or even your car, the space in which you will be spending most of your change-related time is a critical part of your change journey. It needs to support and nurture you so that you can think, feel, dream, and plan for your new state of being.

I had a boss who kept his desk piled high with papers and folders—these spilling over onto nearby bookshelves and even onto the floor. When meeting in his office, there would invariably be a great shuffling of these to make space for everyone, creating chaos while we helped to move the stacks around and he, embarrassed at the last minute reorganization, would be flustered and unfocused as the meetings began. He never cleared his office, though, saying this was his "system," and he felt comfortable and secure in it. Seeing him move around in a confused and flustered state,

I was never convinced he really felt "comfortable" with this state. Familiar, probably—comfortable, no.

Most of us are so familiar with the spaces we occupy most that we don't notice how they impact our moods and emotions. It's wise to bring this to awareness—our environments greatly impact us.

I highly recommend starting your change journey with a pristine, new backdrop for your transformed life. As far as your resources allow, clean, organize, and even redecorate your work space, your bedroom, your home—whatever the environment where most of your change will occur or where the planning will occur.

Creating Your Change Environment

Clarify: Decide what you want to do in your space. Will you need a desk and computer? A whiteboard for planning? A phone? Will it include a meditation corner or space for visitors? Will you want to watch movies and TV, listen to music, or do you want complete silence? Will you want space for exercise or refreshments? Will you want a space with lots of windows or a cozy room with complete privacy?

Design: Draw out your new desired space, describing in detail the furniture you want, the flooring, lighting, wall colors, seating, and other materials. There are many aspects to consider. I think that the three most important are creating good flow, keeping your environment healthy, and choosing the colors and scents that help you achieve your goals.

Identify the Space: Once you know how you want to use your space, find or create that space or room. Once you have the room, take stock of what's in it. Do you need additional items? Make a list based on your vision for the entire space.

Plan: Make a plan for how to put your changes in place by creating a set of SMART goals (see chapter 5). Be very specific and attach all steps to dates. If you need to hire people or ask for friends to help you, include their timing in your plan. Also evaluate your budget and things for which you need others' permission or help. For example, you might be renting your space. If so, will you need permission to paint, wallpaper, add shelving or other storage space, or change the flooring? For those things not within your control, decide how to work around them. For example, if your space has few windows and your vision includes a lot of natural light, you might want to consider switching spaces if you can or adding UV lights.

Be patient. If you cannot achieve all the elements of your desired space right away, do it in phases and take action a few steps at a time.

Create Good Flow

The ancient philosophical practice of fêng shui, which originated in China, translates in English to "wind water."[30] It is a system for placing buildings and orienting objects and furniture within a building to ensure the energy will be able to flow without becoming blocked and establishing a method by which any negative energies can be released. The proper use of fêng shui is believed to bring good fortune.

The following are some of its basic principles, which you can include in the design of your change space:

- As you enter your space, the far-left corner is your wealth and prosperity corner. This is a good place for a small tabletop fountain, a valuable item, or even an affirmation. Blues, purples, and reds are the colors of prosperity. Can you include these colors in something that makes you feel prosperous?

- Locate a home office close to the front of the property and to the front door, but it can be on a different floor. This area is recommended because a lot of energy can flow in to inspire you. Place your desk in the farthest corner so that you can always have a view of the entire room and the entrance.

- Keep entrances free of clutter and dirt.

- In a work space, place your desk in a position that allows you to see the door of your office and be sure that your back is supported by the wall. This is the power position.

- Position your computer strategically: on the west side of your desk to enhance creativity and on the southeast side to generate income.

- Keep your work space separate from the bedroom. Work energy and sleep energy conflict with each other. If you have no choice because you live in a studio or a small apartment, try to partition off your work area with a screen.

- Stay up to date with repairs and replacements. Broken light bulbs, rickety chairs, scratched desks—all these things represent blockages in the energy of the office.

- Integrate organic materials and representations of nature into your work space to help build trust. Wicker baskets, wooden trays, crystal paperweights, ceramic mugs, and potted plants will encourage people to let down their guard with you.

- Place symbols of good fortune—dragon, phoenix, unicorn, and turtle—in your work space.

- Avoid any clutter on surfaces and keep files and tools out of your way. This will allow the energy and creativity to flow while you work.

- Natural elements are important to our well-being. Fêng shui principles recommend that we use water to inspire communication, metal to encourage prosperity, earth to promote long-standing relationships and balance in the workplace, fire to boost productivity, and wood to allow your creativity to flow.

Color Your World

The impact of color on human emotion and psychology is studied intensely by marketers, product manufacturers, educators, and others interested in motivating people to do or feel certain things.[31]

Others have found that color can even change behaviors. For example, in 2000, the city of Glasgow, Scotland, installed blue street lights in certain neighborhoods to improve the city's landscape. They noticed greatly reduced crime and suicide rates. (Blue is known for its calming effect.[32])

How color influences a person depends on many factors, including individual differences, such as gender, age, and culture. Be aware of how certain colors impact you when deciding on your change environment.

Recent studies have shown that when exposed to blue and green hues,[33] a person's heart rate drops, blood pressure lowers, and muscles relax, while hot colors, like red or orange, cause these values to rise. Greens and blues are used in bedrooms, bathrooms, hospitals, test centers, and television stations to ease nerves and other harsh emotions as well as to create a peaceful feeling.

Whether this reaction has to do with the effect of wavelengths on brain chemistry, linguistic associations, cultural meanings, or coincidence has yet to be fully determined.

A color scheme that incorporates warm colors encourages people to linger, which is why many restaurants are decorated in deep burgundy, burnt orange, and other similar colors. These colors stimulate warmth and comfort, and when people relax over a meal, they are more likely to enjoy a leisurely dessert or a cup of coffee.

Scents of Change

Certain scents have proven benefits for stress relief, energy, focus, and overall health.[34] You can test these out for yourself and include some in your change environment. They come in a variety of forms, including candles, dried herbs, sachets, oils, and infusions. Following are some of the most popular:

For Calm and Sleep

Lavender: Lavender has been used as an antiseptic as well as for mental-health purposes. According to a study, lavender used for aromatherapy slows down the activity of the sympathetic nervous system, the body system that responds to stress. This allows improved quality of sleep and relaxation, mood stability, and more focused concentration.

Chamomile: Studies show that chamomile has antispasmodic and anti-inflammatory effects. It also has antibacterial, antifungal, and antiviral properties. Chamomile tea has a calming effect for irritability and insomnia, congestion, and cough.

Bergamot: The fresh lemon, citrus, or orange scent of the extracted oil, when blended with other scents, will not just aid in digestion or inflammation, but it has also shown to be useful in treating depression as well as uplift and refresh the anxious person.

Sandalwood: From ancient times up to today, the most important use of sandalwood is its sedative effect on the nervous system. Researchers discovered that when a person is allowed to smell the scent, brain waves relax. Sandalwood pacifies anxiety, anger, and rage, and it induces sleep.

Mandarin: Psychological studies have shown that mandarin creates a hypnotic effect for those who are anxious and nervous. Moreover, it has a strengthening effect for those who are depressed and grieving.

Jasmine: This is my favorite plant, flower, and scent! "King of the Garden," "Mistress of the Night," and "Moonlight of the Grove" are some nicknames for these wonderful, small white flowers. Their fragrance has captured poets' imaginations and perfumers' fancies since ancient times. Studies have revealed that the scent of jasmine enhances mental alertness as well as stimulates brain waves. Its rich floral fragrance, with an undertone of fruit, is used as an antidepressant, allowing those who are sad to be uplifted since it induces warm and calming emotions. Jasmine also provokes sensuous qualities.

Vanilla: The scent of vanilla is often associated with food, ice creams, cakes, pastries, and chocolates. It has a calming, relaxing, and comforting effect.

Rose: The rose flower and petal earned it the title "Queen of the Garden." For poets and lovers, roses symbolize love and perfection. The wonderfully intense, sweet, and floral scent is one of the most renowned in the world. Useful in calming nervous tensions, it is considered a cell rejuvenator and rebalances the psyche, giving one a positive feeling about oneself.

Hosur, Tamilnadu, India

Lilac: Lilac is known as a flower of love. Its scent brings serenity, pleasurable memories, and peaceful slumber.

Ylang-ylang: The intensely sweet, heady, floral, and spicy scent of ylang-ylang has both stimulating and calming effects. For some, ylang-ylang induces sleep. However, according to research, it stimulates mental alertness. For many, sniffing the extract of this flower lowers blood pressure and relieves palpitations. For those who are anxious or angry, ylang-ylang is known for its ability to slow down the sympathetic nervous system.

Keep Your Environment Healthy

On any given day, do you experience itchy eyes, skin rashes, stuffy and runny noses, fatigue, aches and pains, or sensitivity to odors? If so, it's likely they are caused by allergens in your office or at home. Even if you don't think of yourself as an allergic person, odds are, you could be susceptible. One in five people in the United States have either allergy or asthma symptoms, and more than half of the US population tests positive for one or more allergens. Allergies rank fifth on the list of chronic diseases in the United States.[35]

Your home or office could be "sick," a term first coined in the 1970s to refer to spaces with allergens causing their inhabitants some of the above symptoms.[36]

Combined with the impact of stress on the body, the process of change makes you even more vulnerable to environmental allergens. When you're stressed out, your body releases hormones and other chemicals, including histamine, the powerful chemical that leads to allergy symptoms. While stress doesn't actually cause allergies, it can make an allergic reaction worse by increasing the histamine in your bloodstream. Conversely, allergy symptoms can make you feel further stressed.

When you create your change space, the following are some tips for keeping it allergy free:

- Filter the indoor air. Cover air conditioning vents with cheesecloth to filter pollen and use high efficiency particulate air filters. Clean air filters frequently and air ducts at least once a year.

- Keep the humidity in your house below 50 percent to prevent mold growth. Install dehumidifiers in basements and other areas where moisture is prone to collect.

- Don't allow smoking in the spaces you occupy most often.

- Wear a mask and gloves when cleaning, vacuuming, or painting to limit dust and chemical exposure.

- Make sure there is an exhaust fan over the stove to remove cooking fumes.

- If you have pets, consider keeping them outside. Animal dander and saliva are common allergens for many people. If you must keep your pets indoors, do not allow them in the bedroom and be sure to bathe them often.

- Avoid spending a lot of time in areas where mold may collect, including basements, garages, crawl spaces, barns, and compost heaps. Clean these areas often.

- Wash shower curtains and bathroom tiles with mold-killing solutions.

- Don't collect too many indoor plants since soil encourages mold growth.

- Store firewood outside.

- Limit throw rugs to reduce dust and mold. If you do have rugs, make sure they are washable.

- When possible, choose hardwood floors instead of carpeting. If you must have carpeting, choose a low-pile material.

- Avoid dust-collecting Venetian blinds or long drapes. Replace old drapes with window shades.

Check with your physician for advice and treatment regarding any allergy symptoms you might have.

Chicago, Illiinois, USA

8. INSPIRATION

I'm not going to make everybody happy. And anybody who wants to hate is going to hate. You have to be confident in who you are and what you're doing. Of course you try to evolve. I would never tell you, "Today is the best I will ever be." I'm always trying to be a better chef, a better dad, a better person.

—*Guy Fieri*

Every once in a while, especially during times of change, each of us wakes up to a day we just cannot face—not one more interview, not one more rejection, not one more minute of conversation with a difficult person, and not one more second of uncertainty. You feel tired, old, beaten, discouraged, and alone. Everyone gets to that point at some time. When it happens, take time out to check in with your emotional and physical self as we've discussed in the previous chapter.

I've include quotes throughout this book, which I hope you find inspirational. Here are some additional ones, which you can use as mantras or focal points to help ride out any tough times along your change journey, and to keep you energized. Add your own and keep them handy.

Mantras and Quotes

This, too, will pass.

For every uphill, there is a downhill.

I have successfully met other challenges in my life—I will be successful now.

Other people, including people I admire and emulate, are, at this very minute, facing what I'm facing. I am not alone.

I have love and support.

I am living not by human laws, but by divine ones. My every need is met.

I have abundance on all levels.

If I've ever been [rich, thin, happy, successful, beloved, recognized, energetic, competitive, famous, award winning—fill in your desired attributes], I am still those. All I have ever been, or ever will be, I am now.

Then I saw a new heaven and a new earth; for the first heaven and the first earth had passed away, and the sea was no more and I heard a loud voice from the throne saying, "Behold, the dwelling of God is with men. He will dwell with them, and they shall be his people," and God himself said, "Behold I make all things new." (Revelation 21:1–8)

When coasting downhill, moving fast and easily with your breath flowing in and out, use the momentum to continue moving the same way once the ground is level—or even if the road turns uphill.

"What would be the point in living if we didn't let life change us?" (Julian Fellows, writer, Downton Abbey)

La Jolla, California USA

Find more quotes and inspiration at communication-leadership-change.com.

References for Further Study

1. Kurt Lewin, John Kotter, Daniel Goleman, Warner Burke, and Marvin Weisbord are among the pioneers and stalwarts of the field of organization development (OD), with many research studies and books published about change, leadership, and growth. Dr. Peter Sorensen and Dr. Therese Yaeger serve as dean and associate dean of Benedictine University's School of Management's organization behavior program. See: Goleman, Daniel, *Emotional Intelligence: Why It Can Matter More than IQ* (New York: Bantam Books, 2005).

2. Kurt Lewin, "Frontiers of Group Dynamics: Concept, Method and Reality in Social Science, Social Equilibria, and Social Change," *Human Relations* (1947): 1, 5–41.

3. John P. Kotter, *Leading Change* (Boston: Harvard Business Review Press, 1996).

4. Ludwig Von Bertalanffy, *General System Theory: Foundations, Development, Applications*, rev. ed. (New York: Penguin University Books, 1969).

5. D. Katz and R. Kahn, *The Social Psychology of Organizations* (New York: Wiley, 1966).

6. Joseph Luft and Harry Ingham, *The Johari Window: A Graphic Model for Interpersonal Relations* (University of California Western Training Lab, 1955).

7. Robert Fulghum, *All I Really Need to Know I Learned in Kindergarten: Uncommon Thoughts On Common Things* (New York: Ballantine Books, 1988); Dale Carnegie, *How to Win Friends and Influence People* (New York: Simon and Schuster, 1981).

8. Henry Kimsey-House, Karen Kimsey-House, Phillip Sandahl, and Laura Whitworth. *Co-Active Coaching: Changing Business, Transforming Lives*, 3rd ed. (Boston: Nicholas Brealey Publishing, 2011).

9. David Cooperrider & Associates. "Appreciative Inquiry," http://www.davidcooperrider.com/tag/appreciative-inquiry, Accessed 11 March, 2016.

10. Aaron Beck, "History of Cognitive Behavior Theory, http://www.beckinstitute.org/history-of-cbt/. Accessed 23 January 2016.

Judith S. Beck and Aaron T. Beck. *Cognitive Behavior Therapy: Basics and Beyond*, 2nd ed. (New York: Guilford Publications, 2011).

11. Lynn Grabhorn. *Excuse Me, Your Life is Waiting* (Charlottesville: Hampton Roads Publishing, 2000).

Og Mandino. *The Greatest Salesman in the World* (Bantam Books, 1968).

12. Shakti Gawain, *Living in the Light: A Guide to Planetary Transformation* (San Rafael: New World Library, 1986).

13. "The Burden of Stress in America," http://www.rwjf.org/en/research-publications/find-rwjf-research/2014/07/the-burden-of-stress-in-america.html.

14. Karl Albrecht, *Stress and the Manager: Making It Work for You* (New York: Simon and Schuster, 1979).

American Institute of Stress, http://www.stress.org/workplace-stress.

Thomas Bradbury, "Couple's Best Strategies for Managing Stress." http://www.pbs.org/thisemotionallife/blogs/ couples%E2%80%99-best-strategies-managing-stress.

Joseph P. Folger, Marshall Scott Poole, and Randall K. Stutman, *Working Through Conflict: Strategies for Relationships, Groups, and Organizations* (New York: Pearson Education Publishing, 2013).

Women's Success Coaching, http://womenssuccesscoaching.com/2012/01/13-tips-to-build-assertive-communication-skills.

15. "Selye's General Adaptation Syndrome." http://www.integrativepro.com/Resources/Integrative-Blog/2014/General-Adaptation-Syndrome-Stages. Accessed 12 June, 2016.

16. John J. Ratey and Eric Hagerman, *SPARK: The Revolutionary New Science of Exercise and the Brain* (New York: Little, Brown and Company, 2013).

"Exercise and stress: Get Moving to Manage Stress," April 16, 2015, http://www.mayoclinic.org/healthy-lifestyle/stress-management/in-depth/exercise-and-stress/art-20044469.

"Exercise for Stress and Anxiety," July 2014,

http://www.adaa.org/living-with-anxiety/managing-anxiety/exercise-stress-and-anxiety.

National Institute of Mental Health Science News, "Stress-Defeating Effects of Exercise Traced to Emotional Brain Circuit," June 9, 2011, http://www.nimh.nih.gov/news/science-news/2011/stress-defeating-effects-of-exercise-traced-to-emotional-brain-circuit.shtml.

17. "Who Was Edgar Cayce?" http://www.edgarcayce.org/. Accessed 29 July 2016.

18. "5 Reasons to Spend More Time Outside—Even When It's Cold," March 06, 2015, http://fitness.mercola.com/sites/fitness/archive/2015/03/06/spending-time-outdoors.

19. "5 Reasons to Spend More Time Outside—Even When It's Cold." (See above.)

"Vitamin D and Depression. Where is all the Sunshine?" 2011, http://www.ncbi.nlm.nih.gov/pmc/articles.

"Vitamin D—One of the Simplest Solutions to Wide-Ranging Health Problems," December 22, 2013, http://articles.mercola.com/sites/articles/archive/2013/07/01/vitamin-d-benefits.

Health Benefits of Sunshine. http://www.mensjournal.com/health-fitness/health/the-health-benefits-of-sunshine-20140630.

20. "5 Reasons to Spend More Time Outside—Even When It's Cold." (See above.)

21. "5 Reasons to Spend More Time Outside—Even When It's Cold.," (See above.)

22. "How Much Sleep Do You Need?" https://sleepfoundation.org/how-sleep-works/how-much-sleep-do-we-really-need.

"Electronics in the Bedroom: Why it's Necessary to Turn off Before You Tuck In." https://sleepfoundation.org/ask-the-expert/electronics-the-bedroom.

23. "What Are Adaptogens and Their Superhealth Benefits?" http://www.superfoods-for-superhealth.com/what-are-adaptogens.html.

Frank Lipman, "Adaptogens: Nature's Miracle Anti-stress and Fatigue Fighters," November, 2014, http://www.drfranklipman.com/adaptogens-natures-miracle-anti-stress-and-fatigue-fighters.

These are just two sources among many research and popular articles about adaptogens. An online search will direct you to them.

24. "Effect of Green Tea on Reward Learning in Healthy Individuals: a Randomized, Double-Blind, Placebo-Controlled Pilot Study," *Nutrition Journal* 18 (June 2013).

25. "Long-Term Effects of a Very Low-Carbohydrate Diet and a Low-Fat Diet on Mood and Cognitive Function," 2009. JAMA Internal Medicine

26. "Mood Food—Chocolate and Depressive Symptoms in a Cross-Sectional Analysis." 2010. JAMA Internal Medicine.

27. "Guided Imagery," http://acadgi.com/abouttheacademy/howimageryworks/index.html.

"Meditation: A Simple, Fast Way to Reduce Stress," July 19, 2014, http://www.mayoclinic.org/tests-procedures/meditation/in-depth/meditation/art-20045858.

Sue McGreevey. "Meditation's Positive Residual Effects," *Harvard Gazette,* November 13, 2012, http://news.harvard.edu/gazette/story/2012/11/meditations-positive-residual-effects.

28. Maud Purcell, "The Health Benefits of Journaling," http://psychcentral.com/lib/the-health-benefits-of-journaling.

Bridget Murray, "Writing to Heal," *Monitor on Psychology* 33, no. 6 (2002): http://www.apa.org/monitor/jun02/writing.

Psychology Today, http://www.psychologytoday.com/blog/sense-and-sensitivity/201303/journaling-provides-stress-relief-hsps.

29. "Clutter's Effects on Your Life and Health," 2010, http://redlotusletter.com/clutters-effects-on-your-life-how-clutter-affects-you-and-what-to-do-about-it.

30. "Feng Shui at Home," http://relaxationathome.com/feng-shui-at-home.

"Feng Shui and Stress Relief. What is Feng Shui and How Does It Impact Stress?" http://stress.about.com/od/stressmanagementglossary/g/What-Is-Feng-Shui-And-How-Does-It-Impact-Stress.htm.

Udemy (Feng Shui), https://www.udemy.com/blog/feng-shui-bagua.

Veria, http://www.veria.com/wellness/feng-shui-for-the-workplace.

31. "Stress-Reducing Colors," http://www.huffingtonpost.com/2013/04/18/stress-reducing-colors_n_3102683.html.

"Psychological Effects of Colors," http://www.colour-affects.co.uk/psychological-properties-of-colours.

Kendra Cherry, "Color Psychology: How Colors Impact Moods, Feelings, and Behaviors," Accessed April 16, 2016, https://www.verywell.com/color-psychology-2795824.

32. John M. Grohol, "Can Blue-Colored Light Prevent Suicide? World of Psychology," http://psychcentral.com/blog/archives/2008/12/13/can-blue-colored-light-prevent-suicide.

33. "The Color Psychology of Blue," May 9, 2016,

https://www.verywell.com/the-color-psychology-of-blue-2795815.

"Color Psychology—Green," July 15, 2015, https://www.verywell.com/color-psychology-green-2795817.

34. "Aromatherapy and Essential Oils," http://www.everydayhealth.com/health-center/aromatherapy-and-essential-oils-pdq-complementary-and-alternative-medicine-health-professional-information-nci.aspx.

"Aromatherapy," www.aromaweb.com. Accessed 30 November, 2015.

35. "Allergy Statistics and Facts," http://www.webmd.com/allergies/allergy-statistics.

WebMD, "Stress and Allergies," http://www.webmd.com/allergies/features/stress-and-allergies.

"National Institutes of Health," http://www.niehs.nih.gov/health/topics/conditions/asthma/allergens.

"Everyday Health," http://www.everydayhealth.com/allergy-pictures/top-6-environmental-allergies.aspx.

36. "What is Sick Building Syndrome?" http://www.ei-resource.org/illness-information/related-conditions/sick-building-syndrome/.

ABOUT THE AUTHOR: JAYA KOILPILLAI BOHLMANN

MSMOB, Management, Organizational Behavior
MA, Communication
APR, Public Relations

With more than twenty years of experience in communication and change management with individuals and all types of organizations, Jaya Koilpillai Bohlmann has seen firsthand the challenges related to change. Seeing it done well and done poorly, she is committed to helping people manage the pain and uncertainty related to creating a new future, moving sometimes only on faith. Jaya is a recognized thought leader in the fields of communication and organization development, frequently speaking and writing on change, communication, and related topics. She is involved with several communication and organizational behavior professional organizations and is a founding executive member of a family-run nonprofit dedicated to social, health, and economic issues of children and families in India (www.cupinternational.org).

As a wife, mother, and executive, Jaya has firsthand experience and insight about what it takes to navigate change from the unique perspectives, responsibilities, and roles that are put on and taken on by women. She is a champion for women of all ages, and this book is a special message of hope and knowledge for them.

Personally, Jaya has learned to tolerate change and even instigate it when the time is right. Drawing from her experiences and from those around her, she shares a wealth of knowledge about change, with the understanding that it is the wave that buoys us up, keeps us afloat, carries us into deep, unknown waters—and then home to the shore.

Contributions

Dr. John Bohlmann, N.D. studied naturopathic medicine at the renowned National University of Health Sciences in Lombard, Illinois. He has drawn on his knowledge of biomedical sciences, engineering, psychology of consciousness, applied kinesiology, nutrition, herbal medicine, homeopathy, psychosocial behavior, hypnotherapy, spirituality, genetics, environmental medicine, and the general community of medical professionals to establish a strong understanding of the way our spirit, mind, and body interact with the environment.

About the Photographs - *Note from the Author*

These images are those I've captured during my travels to the places where I have found support, inspiration, healing, imagination, and, above all, love. The air, the earth, the sounds, and the aromas of India speak to me as eternal, ageless, mystical, and healing. In nature, every instant carries change—nothing is constant, quiet, or still. I include them in the book to further carry the spirit of *This Changes Everything.*

This Changes Everything: Transforming Your Life From the Inside Out

Copyright © 2017 by Jaya Koilpillai Bohlmann

All rights reserved.

ISBN 978-0-692-29692-9

www.ingramcontent.com/pod-product-compliance
Lightning Source LLC
Chambersburg PA
CBHW070548090426
42735CB00013B/3112